Street Parables for Today

Street Parables for Today

Keith Tondeur

Authentic

Copyright © 2004 Keith Tondeur

08 07 06 05 04 7 6 5 4 3 2 1

First published 2004 by Authentic Media,
9 Holdom Avenue, Bletchley, Milton Keynes, Bucks,
MK1 1QR, UK
and PO Box 1047, Waynesboro, GA 30830-2047, USA

British Library Cataloguing in Publication Data

A catalogue record for this book is available from the
British Library

1-86024-514-5

Illustrations by Anthony Trimmer
Cover design by Peter Barnsley
Print Management by Adare Carwin
Printed in Denmark by Nørhaven Paperback A/S

Contents

This book is dedicated to my beautiful wife Sue

Foreword

Keith Tondeur has a great gift for simplifying life's problems – that is why he is so good at showing people how they can clear their financial debts – something for which he is always in great demand for the weeks of the annual New Wine family conferences.

Here Keith is using the same helpful gift, showing how Jesus illustrated life's problems some two thousand years ago by spelling out down-to-earth parables. He updates them to clarify their meaning for the man-in-the-street who may not be so familiar with rural practices: ways of farming, shepherding, fishing or are unacquainted with the customs of eastern domesticity. This is all good stuff and very welcome when growing ignorance prevails today about what the Bible has to say about life.

At the time when Jesus actually used his parables, they were rapidly spread about by word of mouth, and 'the common people heard him gladly'. These *Street Parables* by Keith Tondeur make it easy for ordinary folk today to hear home truths gladly, to accept life's challenges honestly and to pass them on easily. The practical insights about life have been presented so simply and clearly.

This book would make an excellent present for a friend, an easy read for the coffee table, the waiting room or the bedside shelf.

Bishop David Pytches

Introduction

Writing this book has been a real challenge! Having made a decision to follow Christ nearly twenty-five years ago and having read the parables on many occasions, I realized I had not fully understood the depth of what Jesus is saying to us through them. They can be really challenging and at times even appear deeply offensive to us. In fact, I have come to the conclusion that if I have not been shaken by the message behind the story, I probably haven't really understood the message!

Jesus had all kinds of people in his audience, and he wanted everyone to get the point of the eternal truths that he was teaching. To this end he would tell stories that all his listeners could relate to. Whether his audience was rich or poor, well read or illiterate, he wanted the message to get across. This in itself would have been enough to irritate some of the wealthier and learned men listening to him, who would have believed that they were superior to those around them and did not need to hear truths in 'childish' story form. How embarrassing for them to realize, as the tales unfolded, that they themselves were an obstacle preventing others from finding faith.

The parables related to events that people would be familiar with in their own lives, and to subjects that they knew about. At times the stories were pithy and punchy, very much 'in your face': in some cases humour was used to ram the message home. I have tried to do the same and I leave you to determine whether I have had any success at this or not.

The key to reading this book is, as with all of Jesus' teaching, not to be offended or feel condemned. But it is perfectly all right to be deeply challenged! Yes, there may well be times when you feel pretty uncomfortable while reading this. I'm not sure whether this will be of any comfort to you, but I felt so unworthy at one stage that I actually stopped writing for three months. It is easy for us to feel, as Christians, that we have arrived and have all the answers. It is also too easy for us to focus on certain parts of our faith and ignore other parts which are a bit too close to our comfort zone. Perhaps we need to start reading those passages that we skip over regularly and rapidly as we head for the verses we like and have underlined five times in our Bible!

We live in a materialistic society, and it is interesting to reflect on just how many of Jesus' parables deal with the issue of money and with having the right priorities in our lives. It is clear that Jesus is well aware of all the trappings with which the false god of money can tempt us. His words show us that he recognizes what a struggle it will be for many of us to let go of the desire for more, bigger and better things. He has some strong words for us as we stay securely in the opulent surroundings of our comfort zones in the west. Yet we choose to ignore these words at our peril.

There are also many messages here which can help us to grow and can significantly deepen our faith. Above all, there is real hope and real joy available to us as we take

on board what Jesus has to say to us and then gladly let
him lead us as he works out his perfect plans in our lives.
We will be eternally grateful that we do so.

1. Ready or Not

Matthew 24:42–51, Mark 13:32–37

Keep on the lookout and be ready, because you will have no warning before Jesus returns. If you want to understand what this means, take a look at these stories.

If the owner of a house knew when a thief was coming, he would keep watch, inform the police, and do everything he could to ensure that his house was not broken into. You need to be as ready as this, because Jesus will be coming back at a time when you least expect him.

Who, then, is the faithful and obedient foreman whom the gang-master has put in charge of the workers in the fields to ensure that they all get fed and paid at the proper time? It will be good for the foreman when the gang-master returns and finds him faithfully carrying out his duty. He will certainly be promoted. But suppose the foreman thought to himself, 'This is great. The boss is away for a long time. I think I can easily cream off some of this money and food from the workers. I'll take more for myself and have a good time.' In this case it is likely that the gang-master will return unexpectedly and find the foreman drunk and absent from his job. The workers will be upset, hungry and resentful. On seeing this, the gang-master's anger will explode and the foreman will be thrown out with no hope of ever getting his former position back.

Keep short accounts

This story is begging us not to be complacent. We must not treat lightly the greatest gift that any human can possibly receive. Nor can we carry on living day by day as if things will always be the same as they are now. But most importantly, the parable is telling us we must be ready to be accountable *now*. R.T. Kendall has famously said that a clear sign of spiritual growth is that we keep short accounts. This means that the gap between when we sin and when we repent of that sin needs constantly to be getting smaller. So if we have upset someone and we know we need to put it right, it is no good saying, 'I must get round to writing to so-and-so one day and telling him it was my fault.' As soon as we realize we need to do something, we need to pick up the phone or, if at all possible, go to see them in person. It needs to be done straight away. You or the person you want to say sorry to could be struck down by a bus this very day: then the issue would never be sorted out and the surviving party could carry hurts for years.

Similarly, we know that Jesus is coming back one day. It could be in ten thousand years' time. It could be today. It could be in the next five minutes. We will not be able to say, 'Can you come back next week? I've still got a few things to sort out!'

The faithful Christian can look forward to Christ's return with eager anticipation. But the one who has been thinking that this won't happen in his lifetime or that he has years to put things right may well subconsciously be developing an attitude of 'when the cat's away the mice will play'.

By holding short accounts and being ready we will avoid the danger of falling into this trap.

MOTHER OF THE BRIDE.

2. Top Table

Luke 14:7–14

Isn't it funny how some people like to be noticed? How they always want to hog the limelight? This might be you, and on occasions I fear it is me: we need to pay close attention to this story.

When someone invites you to a party, don't take a seat at the top table, for people who are closer to the person throwing the party may well have been invited. If so, the host who invited both of you will come and say to you, 'This place is reserved. Give this person your seat.' By then, not only will you feel humiliated but also the only places left will be right at the back. It is much better when you arrive to take a place at the back. Then when the host sees you he may well say, 'My friend, what are you doing here? Come with me to a better place.' Then he will be honouring you in front of the other guests. For all those who think highly of themselves will be brought down, but those who humble themselves will be lifted up.

Next time you are having a party do not invite your relatives and friends, because if you do they are bound to ask you back and so you will be repaid. But when you plan your meal invite the unemployed, the elderly and the single parents – then you really will be blessed. Although they will not be able to repay you in kind, you will be blessed in many ways and some of these rewards will last for ever.

Be humble

Jesus always encourages us to be humble. Yet it is very easy and quite natural to want the best things for yourself. That is why there is always a charge for the best seats on the plane or the theatre. But if we somehow feel that we deserve the best and that we have merited it in some way because of our goodness, we may well be in for a shock. Puffing ourselves up and making ourselves look important can easily rebound on us. If this happens in public we will be humiliated – and everyone likes to see self-important people brought down a peg or two.

Jesus warns us that even if we get away with this on earth, we won't when we stand before him. We need to remember that whatever we have achieved on earth is not to do with our own merit. It is purely a matter of the gifts God has bestowed upon us and the opportunities he has given us. Yet we continue to try to 'move up in the world' and we desperately send out signals to others which seem to say, 'Look at me: I am very important!' We attempt to do this by mixing with the 'right' people, going to the 'right' places and wearing the 'right' clothes. The question we have to ask ourselves is: who are we trying to impress? If everything is just right, why does it feel so wrong?

Be happy to serve others

Even when Jesus was about to be taken away to suffer a horrendous death, he did not choose to be waited on hand and foot. He was not like the condemned man who ate a hearty breakfast. No, instead he knelt in front of his friends and washed their dirty feet. He was demonstrating that serving others is more important in God's Kingdom than being served. Jesus could have had all the power and prestige in the world, indeed he was offered this early in his ministry by the devil, but he chose service over status.

The more we serve others, the more God knows he can trust us and the more he will then move us to higher places. But the reason why he does this is not to reward us but to enable us to serve on a bigger scale.

Share with others who have less

The second part of the story also hits home. Who do we mix with, and why? Of course we all have friends that we like to be with and whose company we enjoy, but Jesus wants us to go further. It is only natural to ask friends round and go to their homes on occasions, but that is not practising hospitality – it's just us having a good time! What we are being asked to do is extend our generosity and giving further. We need to try to babysit for the single parent who otherwise would never get out of the house, spend time with the widower and smile at the stranger. Offer to buy a sandwich for those we see begging for food on our streets. These things, which may seem minor to us, can actually be an enormous blessing to others in so many ways. The little unexpected kindnesses will be felt by others and will be seen by God.

But how do we do this? How do we keep humble and stay in touch with everybody? The answer, as always, lies in submitting to the will of God. It means being prepared to go where he calls us and to get involved with people when he tells us to. It is not about putting ourselves down and seeing ourselves as useless. Yes, it is about acknowledging our faults and weaknesses, but it is also about recognizing the gifts God has given us and being prepared to use them as and when God tells us.

The Kingdom of heaven is the most wonderful place and God has freely opened it to all. While we are bound to be closer to some people than to others, we must not exclude people from the party just because they have a different background to ours. God simply calls us to serve others, especially when they are the weakest and most vulnerable members of our society.

3. Sorted

Matthew 13:47–50

The Kingdom of heaven is like a net that was let down into the lake and caught all kinds of fish. When it was full, the fishermen pulled it up on the shore. Then they sat down and collected the good fish in baskets but threw the bad away. This is how it will be at the end of the age. The angels will come and separate the bad from the righteous and they will be thrown into hell, suffering eternal separation from God.

Remember to be grateful, because everyone who has studied God's Word and truly understood about the Kingdom of heaven is like someone who gets many new gifts to add to what he already has.

Witness in the world

We are called to listen to what God says and to tell others about him. If you like, we are to swim in the sea with all the other sorts of fish, both good and bad. We may be very different to non-believers but we are still to be in the world!

Do not judge

It is not our job to judge which category people fit into.
Fortunately this is not our decision and it would be
foolish to try even to guess who is part of the Kingdom
and who is not. This decision will be made by the great
'Fisher of men' at the final judgement and we can safely
leave this to him. Our responsibility is to urge others to
do something about their unsaved state.

Jesus always adds treasure to our lives

The last sentence of the story tells us that Jesus comes to
add that extra special ingredient to what we already
have. Just as every wonderful thing on earth demonstrates there has to be a Creator, so the Old Testament
both confirms the law and points to Jesus as Messiah.
Jesus always confirmed the importance of the law, and at
the same time affirmed that he was indeed the Messiah.
As a result, we now have something new and special – a
real treasure.

The Bible shows us how to live in our world and
teaches us that we need to move forward in ever-
deepening faith. But, as with the Pharisees, it is easy to be
so involved in the rituals of the old that you become blind
to the new things that are happening.

Jesus wants to keep adding gifts to our lives, but more
than anything he wants us to grasp and appreciate the
gift that his death has given to all who acknowledge him
for who he is – life everlasting.

4. Flat Battery

Luke 11:5-10

Suppose one of your neighbours is a friend and you go to
him at three in the morning, saying, 'Pete, please lend me
your jump leads. We are due at the airport in an hour to go
on holiday and the car battery is flat.'

But the answer you get is not what you want to hear.
'Please don't disturb me. I've had a long day at work and
my shift starts again in four hours. Anyway, the kids are all
asleep and the burglar alarm is switched on. Try and get a
taxi.'

Although Pete does not want to get up and give you the
jump leads, even though he is your friend, your
persistence will show that you are serious and that asking
him for help is the only option you have. He will then get
up, lend you what you need and stay with you until he
knows you have left safely.

So, ask seriously and it will be given to you, look
intently and you will find everything you are seeking. Keep
on knocking, because the door will be opened. For
everyone who asks receives, he who looks seriously will
find, and if you keep on knocking, the door will be opened.

God will provide

This is wonderful news. The story does not mean that if
you ask for fifty million pounds hard enough or for long
enough God will give it to you. But it does mean that God
will provide all the resources you need for his purpose to
be fulfilled in your life. You do not have to worry about
not being good enough or being too inexperienced. If he
has asked you to do something, he will pour out the
resources generously and abundantly to ensure you have
everything you need to do an excellent job. This is hard
for us to grasp and we often shy away from doing things
God has called us to do because we don't think we are up
to the job. The simple truth is we aren't, but by relying on
his supernatural resources we are able to do the most
wonderful things.

Life can be disturbing

Can you remember the last time the phone rang in the
middle of the night or a knock on the door disturbed
you? Maybe you were in a deep sleep and the sound
jarred you awake. For a few seconds you haven't got a
clue where you are. There is a moment of anger at
someone disturbing your sleep, but that is rapidly
replaced by the fear that something awful has happened
to a loved one and you are about to hear some distressing
news. Suddenly you are frightened of answering the
phone or going to the door.

   Most of us need and welcome a good night's rest.
Unbroken sleep is a real benefit and to be woken up in
the middle of the night can mean we will get no more
sleep that night. It is especially difficult when you have

the whole family sleeping with you, because even though you are very sleepy you have to respond quickly, or the whole household will soon be wide awake.

But back to the story. The family is up and ready to go on their holiday. They have been looking forward to it for months. Now they are all ready to go to the airport and dear old Dad has let the car battery go flat! Massive apportioning of blame is about to happen. Sheepishly, Dad knows he has to wake his friend next door. There is no time for anything else. He does not want to do it, but he convinces himself that if the roles were reversed he would be magnanimous in such a situation. So he goes and knocks on the door.

At first there would probably be no response. So he would try again a little louder. By now he would know that he would probably be waking the children up and causing much annoyance in the household. But it was all he could do. Eventually he would hear one of the children stirring, calling to his father, 'Dad, there's someone at the door.'

Perhaps the neighbour would open the bedroom window and call out, 'What on earth is it?' On hearing the reply he might feel irritated that he had been woken for something that was not a life or death matter. But then he would realize that if he did nothing the noise would soon wake the whole house. So he would reluctantly stagger out of bed and go to the garage to get the jump leads. Having been asked, he would soon feel concern and want to stay around to ensure that the car did eventually start and the family was able to get off on its holiday on time. By then, he would probably have offered to drive them in his own car if all else failed.

Being good neighbours

What would we have done? Hopefully there are very few of us who would roll over and go back to sleep! The point of the story is that if we sinful, selfish people will eventually respond in such a positive way, how much more will our Father in heaven when we seriously ask him for help? He doesn't go to sleep or have other distractions! He is waiting for and wanting us to speak to him more and more.

It is important to recall that Jesus told his parable just after he had taught the disciples to pray using the Lord's Prayer. Included in this are the words, 'Give us this day our daily bread.' If we ask him he will provide. Yet many of us, and I include myself in this, do not pray as often as we should. In fact prayer can so easily be used as an afterthought. Is this because we see God as a sort of reluctant neighbour, or is it more that we are too busy doing our own thing and trying to achieve things 'my way'? Do we perhaps feel guilty, that we don't deserve what we are asking for? Well, that may be true, but it must not stop us asking.

God is generous

God loves his world and he loves the people in it! This includes you and me. God *wants* to be generous to each of us and is so pleased with us when we, however reluctantly, mirror that generosity to others. His ability to give is always greater than our ability to receive. He rejoices to see his people respond warmly as he answers their prayer. But he wants us to share in that same joy.

This is why he encourages us to help meet the needs of others who have less than we have, so that we too can receive that joy.

Having this 'servant heart' and putting others first is not forced upon us. But as we empty ourselves and ask God to fill us with his good things, so we become more like Jesus, who of his own free will gave up everything for us.

Being grateful

Imagine, for a moment, that it is your birthday and your partner gives you something you have really wanted for years. You would be thrilled, and you would be so careful with it, ensuring it stayed in pristine condition and was used wisely. But you would also tell your partner over and over again how grateful you were, what a really special gift it was and how you would never ever forget such generosity. You would want to show your thanks in many different ways.

Yet God has given us a gift that nothing else can remotely compare with. The more we talk to our Father and thank him for the great gift of Jesus, the happier he is. He is pleased when we grasp what a great cost there was in sending Jesus to earth to die for us. And as we humbly talk to him about our needs, we do not have to keep hammering louder and louder out of fear that he will not hear us or respond to our pleas.

God will answer our prayers. Sometimes this will not be when we had wanted or in the manner we had hoped for, but there are good reasons for this. God knows the bigger picture. He knows what is best for all of us. His timing is always perfect. Can we trust him in this? Sometimes we realize that what we were praying for last year didn't happen because God had much better things in store. He may also be testing our patience, or our commitment to what we are praying about. Our perspective is almost always based on the here and now. God has a viewpoint that stretches into eternity.

So why are some prayers not answered? Why do some people get healed and others not, some people make a commitment to Christ and others appear not to? I have no idea at all, but I am prepared to trust my loving heavenly Father, who I know is making all things good for those who know Christ Jesus. I know he is answering all my prayers in the best way possible, because he is not just a good neighbour, he is a great God!

5. Neighbours

Luke 10:25–37

Many religious people are anxious to find the right formula to ensure that their behaviour and good works gain them eternal life. We know that the Bible clearly says we should love God and our neighbour as much as we love ourselves, and Jesus tells us that through doing this we will have eternal life. But are we really doing this? Take a look at the following story. It might just prompt a bit of self-analysis!

A young girl was coming home from a late night party rather the worse for wear. She was assaulted, beaten, mugged and left in the entrance to an alley. A liberal churchman was going down the main road on the way to church, and when he saw her he passed by on the other side. He was hurrying to a debate about one-hundred-and-one ways to find God. An evangelical also passed by on the other side. He could not possibly be late for his church service, as a few new converts from Alpha could be attending. But a barman from a club saw her and felt pity for her. He stopped his car, went over to her and helped clean up her wounds. He drove her to a nearby hotel he knew, where he asked the manager to look after her and give her a bed and a good meal. He gave the hotel manager his credit card details and told him to charge all the expenses to it.

It was only then that the barman went home and told his long-term partner what had happened. He had been in a homosexual relationship for twenty-three years.

If we were asked which of the three men was a neighbour to the young girl, I am sure we would all say the man who was kind to her. In other words, we are talking about the one who actually did something about her plight.

Jesus clearly concurs with this message. This is correct teaching. We need to look behind the label. We need to show our Christian love and compassion to everyone we come across.

The dangers of being 'religious'

In both versions of this parable recorded in the Bible Jesus is speaking to a 'religious' person. We need to let this sink in. So often we see the Pharisees simply as the 'baddies', the people who turned the crowds against Jesus. But actually they were the religious enthusiasts of the day. They read their Scriptures daily. They tithed and fasted. In their own eyes they were good, model citizens and they believed life would be a lot better if only others followed their example. They regularly communicated with God and it was little surprise, therefore, when 'God told them' various rules that should be obeyed.

Are you feeling uncomfortable yet? Do you ever use the argument 'God told me' when you are in discussion with someone? Have you ever stopped to think how impossible it is to argue back on this one? It is not surprising that some people say this is used as a statement to end a discussion. We must be able to back up our viewpoint through sound argument that is based on biblical foundations.

Our culture and prejudices can affect our thinking

The parables of Jesus were sometimes deeply offensive to his listeners. They were blunt and uncompromising. The conclusions were highly unexpected, and the hero was often the last person the listening crowd would have thought of. If we today can read the parables and not find them deeply challenging, we have probably missed the point! We can think we know the right teaching but it is easy to let our prejudices get in the way. We should recall that in Jesus' day, the Jews despised Samaritans and women were ignored. Yet the first person Jesus spoke to about who he was and about the power of the Holy Spirit was a Samaritan woman. The Jewish scholars of the day believed that their neighbours were only their fellow Jews. Jesus, as always, had a shock for them. He is also asking us today to 'think outside the box' and to remember that we need to be out there mixing with others, sharing with their struggles and pointing them towards him.

Be compassionate

As Christians, we can find that our positions and deeply held beliefs sometimes deflect us from kindnesses. Our determination to keep our passions under control can mean that we also stifle our compassion. It is easy to justify ourselves when situations like this occur, but Jesus is saying to us, 'Hold on a moment. Put yourself in the shoes of the young woman. How grateful you would be to anyone who helped you. Remember: but for the grace of God it could be you lying there in the gutter.'

Why not do that for a moment? Imagine you are the man beaten up by the robbers or think about how you would feel if you were that young girl who had just been attacked. Would you care whether your rescuer was black or white? How about male or female, Christian, Muslim or agnostic, straight or, as in this example, gay? It is so easy for us to see certain people as 'bad' and therefore exclude them as possible heroes. Yet we all fail, and we all sin, so on this basis there can never be a hero. If you were lying there bruised, beaten and bewildered, would you care what label your rescuer had? Surely all that matters is the actions that the various people in the stories take. All the young woman wants is to be helped. She will be very grateful to anyone passing by who stops and comes to her assistance. It is quite likely that as she gets to know more about her rescuer she will start to ask questions: 'Why did you stop? Why have you given up time and money for me? What motivates you to be so kind?'

Love in action

Our faith needs to be love in action. We are called to care for those who are hurting and to do everything in our power to make their situation better. This is not a 'what's in it for me' religion. Yes, it is essential that we have a personal and committed faith, but this means we should always be looking around us. After all, Christ did not die on a pole, concerned about me alone. His arms were nailed to a wooden cross, outstretched as he reached out to a hurting world. Does that reflect our priorities? Do we acknowledge that we are church and our actions say far, far more about us than the fact that we visit a building on Sundays?

I am sure that many of us do feel incensed when thinking about the behaviour of the various people in this parable. But can we be sure we would not do the same? Could we be too busy with other good works to get involved? Could the cost be too great in terms of time, money and effort? Sometimes it is easier to campaign for better policing or lighting, demand stiffer sentences or draw up a petition than to meet the need where it really is.

Being a good neighbour

We need to remember that Jesus would be speaking to a wide audience that included both rich and poor. There would be the religious scholars and the local people side by side. It is perhaps ironic that many followers of Jesus in the western world would fit into the categories of both rich and religious – the two groups that Jesus criticized the most! Are we sure that we are truly loving our neighbour and that 'our' riches are being used his way?

You see, to ask the question 'Who is my neighbour?' condemns us already. The answer is anyone who needs help. True neighbourliness does not look at boundaries. It looks not for limits but for opportunities. People we pass by who are hurting are to do with us. We need to be Jesus to them. It is impossible to define 'neighbour': we can only be one. Barriers of race, sexuality, class and culture do not apply. We need to see everyone as Jesus sees them.

Personal involvement

A good neighbour does things personally. We need to show genuine Christian love in action. There is always a cost to doing this in terms of time, money, effort and prayer. When we give help we give of ourselves, showing the unconditional love of Jesus to a hurting world. Love can only really shine through when life touches life. And as we go down our road, Jesus calls us to act as good neighbours to all we see who have fallen by the wayside. The costs are nothing compared with the cost Jesus paid for each one of us.

We are bombarded in our society with the importance of self, and it is little wonder that we tend to put ourselves first – sometimes even when it comes to our faith. But Jesus calls us to be kind and put others first. Doing this may lead to the scorn of others and we may get emotionally and financially scarred. But we have been set free to show God's unconditional love on earth, to demonstrate that people matter more than things, and that someone else's need is more important than my wants.

Never judge

We also need to be careful about judging others, blaming them for the mess they are in and thinking they have brought these problems on themselves. Can we be sure we would have done any differently? We all do silly things and we all need help on a regular basis. This parable is therefore timeless. It shows that pity that remains just an emotion is in fact a sin. Seeing a need in another must provoke action in us. As churches we can be caught up in ritual or chasing the latest signs and wonders but still be quite dead if we are not offering practical help to our suffering neighbours. Action involves risk; it is about breaking down barriers. It is about deeds and not words; about sacrifice, not respectability. It is about lifestyle and our priorities for the rest of our lives. It is about showing the unconditional love of Jesus to all whom God puts in our path.

6. Excuses

Luke 14:15–24

A church had invited a well-known speaker to come and teach about Jesus. There was considerable excitement among the congregation about his coming and everyone said they were looking forward to it. It was a wealthy church and they wanted to bless the teacher's ministry, so it was agreed that they would charge £20 a ticket for the evening, as he would speak to them after a three-course dinner.

But as the day drew near, people began to make their excuses. One said, 'I've been busy all week. I need to go to the supermarket.' Another said, 'It's the only time I can get my hair done.'

Yet another needed to cut the grass and one had to go to B&Q for some urgent DIY material. Two were test-driving new cars, three were in an important golf match and four always played badminton on that day of the week. Several couples had decided to go out for a meal and others wanted to see a new film. A significant number had to work late at the office.

It soon became clear that hardly any of those from the church who had originally been invited could be bothered to turn up. When this was reported back to the teacher, he asked them to invite people from all the surrounding poorer churches and not to charge. He would come for free and pay for the dinner himself. He personally arranged for caterers to come in and no expense was spared as the meal was prepared. News of this spread quickly around the whole area and on the evening in question the church was full of people really enjoying the banquet laid before them and keenly lapping up every word. They could never have afforded to come and they loved every second. For nearly everyone present it was a life-changing evening and they went away with a much stronger commitment to Jesus.

On the Sunday morning, as the church congregation gathered before the service they gossiped about the various activities they had been involved in during the week. Then they decided to settle down and listen to God for an hour. They could just about give him that amount of time in their busy schedules.

Putting God first

I really do believe that we do not realize how we so readily insult God. He provides great teachers and so many opportunities to learn more about him and worship him. These are opportunities that many Christians in this world can only dream of. Yet so often we find 'good reason' why we cannot go to events that would deepen our faith. The time pressures we are under may even mean that we spend next to no time hearing from him either through his Word or through prayer.

Jesus loved people. He enjoyed their company and was always to be found in the centre at parties. He enjoyed debate with others and welcomed sound teaching. This is why the social side of life is important. If we are expecting people to flock to church so that we can talk to them about our Lord we will have a long wait. We need to be socialising with our non-believing neighbours and finding ways of introducing Christ into our conversations. This must be done as naturally as possible, however!

The teacher realized something we all need to grasp: that what we have is priceless – the gift of eternal life. It is good to be able to share this with others, whatever the cost. Not just to be mixing with our brothers and sisters who have received this Good News already, but urgently seeking out the lost and lonely.

Jesus clearly teaches how easy it is for our own selfish desires and even the busyness of our everyday lives to get in the way of a close relationship with him. But this invitation has eternal importance and should be valued above all else – certainly above the temporary pleasures that money and possessions can bring.

Where does your time go?

Life always seems pressured, but stop and think for a moment (that is, if you have time!). How many hours' overtime have we worked this week? How much time have we spent playing sport? Now, I know that our work and/or children exhaust us, but how long have we spent with God this week? Not going to the church jumble sale and doing things for him, but actually spending time in prayer and conversation with him? After all, doesn't he have perfect plans for our lives? How are we going to know what they are if we never stop to ask him? Is it our busyness or our desire for more money that keeps us from spending more time with him? Perhaps this may

account for why God seems to move much more in the
Third World than he does in the UK.

God is for all

God invites the poor to his banquet, but this is not
because he loathes the rich. Sadly, the very fact that the
poor have been invited can lead to the rich not turning up
at all. We are not superior to others. The more we have,
the more responsibility we bear in using things wisely.
Do we use things his way or our own way?

Rich or poor, good or bad, we are all sinners, but the
rich can easily exclude themselves by demonstrating
through their lifestyle that they have rejected a salvation
that is available to all. We can feel uncomfortable at, or
even scandalized by, the concern Jesus shows for the
poor. It is so easy to shrug our shoulders and do nothing
when we hear of needs: after all, we have some very
important wants of our own. Some will see their riches as
a sign that God favours them and that they will automatically be going to heaven. Others will be outraged
that poor sinners have been invited as well. After all,
heaven is going to be fairly exclusive and white and
middle class, isn't it?!

Putting him first

Please stop and think for a minute. I am assuming that
nearly all of you reading this book believe that Jesus is
the Son of God and that he died to set us free from sin and
assure us of our place in heaven, where we will live for
ever. So are you giving Jesus the time he merits? So often
we can treat our faith as an add-on. We see it as

something little different than going to a golf club or health spa. Church is where we meet our friends on a Sunday, when we can be bothered to show up. Often other things are too important for us to postpone or cancel. And yet every time we ignore God or others made in his image there is Jesus at the side of our Father, saying, 'Father, forgive; Father, forgive.'

The price is cancelled

The rich people in the story want to be able to choose for themselves whether to attend the event, and they also wanted to have a say in who else was being invited. The poor, on the other hand, couldn't believe that they'd been invited. There would never be a way they could afford the price, but the teacher allows them to come entirely free. They love him for it and long to spend time with him and learn more about God. They have understood the message of grace and accepted an invitation they neither expected nor deserved.

It is very easy after we have been Christians for some time for new things to come into our lives and for us to establish new priorities. We need to concentrate on the never-changing goodness of God. Sometimes excuses are valid. Grass does need cutting and so does hair – though not very often in my case! Good things can come between God and us. If it were just bad things it would be so much easier to reject them. But we must never let the good get in the way of the best – our eternal relationship with Jesus.

7. Right Priorities

Matthew 13:44–46

> The Kingdom of heaven is like praying at the bedside of the person you love the most, who is critically ill. All that matters is the recovery of your loved one. All ambition and desire for material things or promotion have vanished. And then the doctor tells you that the patient will make a full recovery. You are so thankful that your priorities change for ever.

Choosing the best

Riches on this earth are meaningless – especially to those of us who profess that Jesus is our Lord and that because of his sacrifices we are going to spend eternity with him.

The Gospel – the Good News – is the chance of a lifetime. We need to respond decisively to it and be willing to give up everything for it, never being prepared to compromise what we have been offered. It should fill us with joy and we should be prepared to sacrifice anything else for it. So often we see our faith as a battle between Good and Evil, between God and the devil, but it does not have to be so. Jesus is telling us that sometimes we need to lay down the good for the best. Just as all of us would surrender anything for the ones we love, so we need to remember there is a cost to following Jesus.

This parable is about events that happen to ordinary people. You can be going about your normal daily routine, looking after the children or earning money, when suddenly the phone rings. One sentence can change your priorities for ever. Close relatives we have not seen for far too long suddenly become important to us as we realize that we may never be able to talk to them again. Parents we have loved but without telling them so since we were small children can suddenly be around no more. We always intended to put our families first but 'things' always got in the way. We 'needed' a new car or that expensive holiday. We will not work such long hours soon. When we stop and reflect, we can soon realize that our priorities are wrong, yet everyday life has a habit of not letting us pause for reflection.

Cling to the best

Now we are Christians, what was previously very important to us should seem inconsequential. We have been chosen – outrageous sinners saved by even more outrageous grace. To get the best we may well be asked to give up things that are now second best. We are called to have radically different priorities. We will need to sacrifice our comfort zone.

The Kingdom of God is priceless but it is also a free gift to all who acknowledge Jesus as Lord. Surrendering everything else naturally means we start taking risks. Jesus is asking us if we are prepared to surrender money, possessions, comfort and security to follow him. The

Kingdom of God is a gift, but this does not mean it is an easy option. We have a treasure far greater than something buried in a field or a precious pearl. Our treasure is even greater than the life of a loved one who knows Jesus, because we know we will spend eternity with them. This is the greatest thing there could ever be, and so we should gladly be sacrificing everything that may get in the way of telling others this wonderful news.

8. Investment Opportunities

Matthew 25:14–30, Luke 19:11–27

We always need to be ready for the imminent return of our Lord Jesus. Here is a story that tells us something of what it will be like.

A man had to go abroad for some time, so he called his managers and asked them to look after his money while he was away. He was aware of their differing abilities, so to one he gave £5,000, to another £2,000 and to a third £1,000. Then he went away. Immediately, one man went to work with his money. Using the £5,000 he had been given he invested wisely, paid close attention to what was happening and was able to double his money. The second worked hard on the land, grew some vegetables and looked after them so well that he, too, was able to double his money from £2,000 to £4,000. But the man who had received the £1,000 did nothing. He simply placed the money in a drawer which he kept locked so that it would not be stolen.

After a while the man returned and asked to see the managers so that he could settle his accounts. The one who had received £5,000 came to him and said, 'Thank you for entrusting the £5,000 to me. I have invested wisely and managed to make £5,000 more.'

The man was delighted. 'Well done!' he said. 'You have been good and faithful with my possessions while I have been away. Since you have been faithful with a small amount I will now trust you with much more. Come with me. I am so grateful to you.'

The man with £2,000 also came and said, 'Thank you. You entrusted £2,000 to me and I put the money to good use, worked hard on the land and was able to gain £2,000 more.'

The owner of the money was delighted. 'Well done!' he said. 'You have been good and faithful with my possessions while I have been away. Since you have been faithful with a small amount I will now trust you with much more. Come with me. I am so grateful to you.'

Then the manager who had received £1,000 came. 'Sir,' he said, 'I know you can be a hard man to please and good things just seem to happen to you. Why, you even seem to get income from places where you haven't invested! Because of this I was afraid, so I just kept your money with me at all times. See, here it is.'

But the owner replied, 'You wicked, lazy good-for-nothing. You know that I look for a return on my investments, which you acknowledge are widely scattered and in many different forms. But you were too idle to use the money I had given you. At the very least you could have put it in a bank where it would have accumulated some interest.'

The owner then took the money from him and gave it to the one who had the £10,000. For everyone who uses the gifts given to him wisely will be given even more. But whoever does not and just wastes what is given to him will find even that taken away. He will then bitterly regret the

opportunities that were given to him but that he was
unprepared to take.

Explanation

In this story different managers were given different
sums to look after, just as we are given different abilities
or 'talents' to fulfil God's purpose. It is not the amount
the manager received or the number of 'talents' we are
given that is important. Rather it is how we utilize God's
gifting that is all-important.

God's gifting

God pours out his gifting onto us and asks that we use it.
By doing so, we will be demonstrating the power of God
in action to those around us who do not believe. But we
will also benefit ourselves because as we draw closer to
God and increasingly do his will, so he in return will
pour out more and more resources to enable us to do, in
his strength, what we have been asked to do.

We need to recognize that God has given us many
things. Not just money and possessions, but time and
characteristics as well. Our 'talents' therefore go beyond
money and relate to absolutely everything that God has
entrusted us with.

Our response

We are just so good at excuses. 'I could never possibly do
that,' 'I'm just not good enough,' or 'I know I don't really

have the necessary skills.' This human response to God echoes through the ages. Look at the early chapters of Exodus and you will see Moses arguing with God: 'You can't really send me,' 'I know they won't believe me,' and 'I am no good at speaking in public.' Moses was too aware of what he didn't have; God was interested in what he could do with him alongside.

Many of us have hidden or latent talents. For all sorts of reasons we tend to keep them locked away. We may have kept them hidden so long that we forget we even have them. Or we leave them, just like an unopened present in a drawer, never letting them see the light of day. We question whether we really have been given such abilities and prefer to hide them away, and thus never achieve all that we could.

To put it rather crudely, God has invested an awful amount in us and he longs to see some return on his investment. In this story the man, the owner of the money, obviously represents God. The managers are you and me, who are called on to be good stewards of his resources. These have been handed to us and it must be our aim to hand them on, or to hand them back if Jesus should return in the meantime, in a better state than when they were first received.

Making a difference

We are called to make things grow; to try to multiply the gifts that God has given us. What we have is of great value, but it is of no value if it is just kept within us and never used. We know, however, that to put it into operation we have to take risks. The man with £5,000 would have found that not all his investments resulted in immediate profit. He would really need to work hard to get his money to double. Similarly, the man working on the land would know that some of his vegetables would not grow properly. He would have to work really hard to get maximum return on his investment. And that is precisely what God our Father wants to see from us. Our potential is there. We all have it in differing amounts and in differing ways. But are we allowing it to be maximized? Are we prepared to take risks, on some occasions to be made to feel foolish and on others to make mistakes for the sake of the Gospel? Or are we more like the man with the £1,000 who was too afraid and therefore too cautious to do anything? His money was locked away. The fear of failure had drowned out the possibility of great success. So in the end his talent was useless. It attracted no interest.

It can be helpful to think of a talent as a coin. On one side is written the word 'gift' and on the other the word 'responsibility'. So for every 'talent' we receive, be it money, possessions or gifting, there is a matching responsibility. It is probably therefore very sensible not to covet what belongs to other people, as we might well fail in our increased responsibilities!

Maximizing our talents

It is good to see that the owner responded to the manager who doubled his money from £5,000 to £10,000 in exactly the same way as he did to the one who doubled his from £2,000 to £4,000. The owner (God) knows our differing abilities and will never ask us to do more than we are capable of. If we achieve this, our rewards will be exactly the same regardless of the amount of 'talent' we are entrusted with.

Please, don't hold back like the man with the £1,000! Be keen and enthusiastic, take risks and share your faith. Don't hide your light under a bushel and please, whatever you do, don't blame your maker! ('I'm too shy. Too impractical. Not clever enough.') Yes, we have extroverts and introverts, people who are good with their brains and others who are very practical. But God has made each one of us as we are, he loves us as we are and he knows just what we are capable of in his strength.

Faith is about growth. It is about going deeper and going forward under the promptings of the Holy Spirit. It is not about the 'good old days'. It is about risking all for Jesus. It is about putting him first and using our talent to help us do so.

So let me try to define our talent. I believe it is everything we are, everything we have and all our abilities. It is our time, money, possessions, family, friendships, work and emotions. It is absolutely everything about you and me.

We should not be like the man who kept his £1,000 talent locked up in a drawer, only remembering it occasionally and, when doing so, feeling dread and a desire to forget about it as soon as possible. We should strive to be like the other two managers. We should not be tied down by obligations but rather liberated by opportunities that will enable us to demonstrate our talents in all sorts of ways.

We should not be content with normality; we should be looking for adventure – to show what God can do through us on every conceivable occasion. Failing to realize that each of us is needed according to our differing abilities can result in paralysis. If one of us is not working to their full potential it can badly impact on the rest of us. If several fail to do so, everything we are trying to achieve can shudder to a halt.

Let's get using our talents!

May I urge you to accept that there is no one who has just one talent? We can all be kind, smile, pray (not necessarily out loud!) and encourage others. God is calling us to do everything we can while we are on earth to use all the talents he has given us at every opportunity. This may seem frightening, but in reality it is exciting! Every talent is needed; none is inconsequential.

As this story demonstrates, we are all accountable to God. The point that it is making is that we should be brave and use the gifts God has given us. If we miss an opportunity, it may be lost for ever.

May I therefore encourage you not to dwell on the abilities you feel you lack, but to improve and develop the talents that have been entrusted to you so that they can make a difference not just now, but for evermore? What is it that you can do so much better than anyone else around? Don't you dare say 'nothing': the possibilities are endless!

The world is not full of multi-talented people and you. You are a multi-talented person. God is not looking for extraordinary people to do extraordinary things; rather he is looking for ordinary people to do ordinary things, extraordinarily well. Do that and one day you too will hear those wonderful words, 'Well done! You have been good and faithful. Come with me. I am so grateful to you.' What an incentive!

9. Welcome Back

Luke 15:11–32

There was a man who had two daughters. The elder, Kate, was content to work through school and go on to university but the younger one, Sally, was restless. 'I'm fed up with living here,' she used to shout at her parents. 'It's so boring. There's nothing to do and my friends never want to go anywhere. As for you, all you do is nag me to death: "Don't go there, don't mix with those people, and don't be late home". You don't love me. You just want to control me.'

Sally, who was fourteen, had seen kids of her age having a great time on the television. She wanted money, things and fun and she wanted them now. Her father had a jeweller's shop in the town where they lived and Sally used to work there on Saturdays. One day she offered to close the shop and bank the takings. Her father worried that she might be up to something as she was so impulsive and wanted things immediately. Obviously she would get a useful inheritance when he died, but if she wanted to take it now he would not stand in her way. So he left the shop early. But rather than do as she had promised, Sally took the cash and all the jewellery and fled north, where she sold it for thousands of pounds.

The money that she had with her enabled her to buy an extensive range of designer label clothes. She changed her hairstyle and had some body piercing and tattoos done. When she looked at herself in the mirror she did not recognize the little girl she had left behind. She was a young woman now, she proudly thought to herself. I don't need my dad to tell me what to do. Sally made friends by showering them with free clothes and drinks and it wasn't long before a man in his twenties took a keen interest in her. Soon they were living together in a flat that she was paying for. Within days he had taken over her life and started to control her money.

Sally lived like this every day, or more appropriately every night, throughout the summer. Her lover introduced her to drugs, soft ones to begin with, but she was soon hooked on crack. Not surprisingly, the lack of sleep and increased drug use were both tiring and very expensive. By the end of the summer Sally realized that she was rapidly running out of money and she noticed that as this was happening all her so-called friends were disappearing just as fast. Soon only the man she loved was left. One day he announced in a matter of fact way that the money had run out and so she would have to start sleeping with men for money.

Sally spent her fifteenth birthday satisfying the perverted needs of a string of men. Older and sicker now because of the drugs and the degradation she was subjected to, she thought life could not get any worse than this. It was then that the man she believed loved her walked through the door with a new, 'fresher' model and she was simply thrown out onto the street. All she had were the clothes that she was just about wearing.

Weeping, she huddled in a shop doorway, pulling some newspaper over herself to try to keep warm. As she did so, the name of her home town sprang out at her from the paper. Suddenly Sally came to her senses. 'I know I have blown it totally with my father,' she thought, 'but if I go back home at least I can be taken into care and get some medical attention. At the very least I must let my dad know I am alive.'

Twice when she rang home she got the answering machine. The third time she left a message. 'Dad, Mum. It's me. It's Sally. I'm so sorry for all the trouble I must have caused. I know I've blown it, but at least in my home town I can be taken into care and hopefully resurrect my school career. I'm going to be on a train that arrives tomorrow. Sorry once more. I will write to you when I'm there and explain to you all the terrible things I've done and what has happened to me.'

Sally had to do one last trick to get the train fare home. Soon she was recognizing the outskirts of her home town and she realized what she had thrown away. The train was pulling into the station now. It stopped and Sally stepped out.

Down the platform she could see her friends and then her mum and dad. Sally knew she had changed her appearance so much that no one would ever recognize her, but in the split second it took for her dad to see her he set off running down the platform as fast as he could go and swept her into his arms. Sally was crying but through her tears she saw that her dad was crying too. She tried to say 'sorry' but was smothered in kisses.

Again Sally tried to apologize. 'I don't deserve to have you here. I've done terrible things. I rebelled against you even though you loved me so much. I wanted money and nice things and I wanted it all immediately. I even wished you dead so I could get my hands on them.'

But her father turned and called to her friends. 'Quick, come. Bring the new clothes we've bought her. Take her to the hairdressers and let her smarten herself up. Spare no expense.' Then, turning to his daughter, he said, 'Every day since you left I've been searching for you, doing everything I could to find you. I'm so glad you've come back. Look, I have a ring to give you that was my mother's. Before she died she told me to give one to Kate and one to you when you had grown up. I think that day has arrived for you today. Now hurry. You don't want to be late for the party!'

As soon as Sally's dad had got the phone message telling him that his younger daughter was coming back, he had rung up Kate at university. With great joy he told her about the phone call and asked Kate to come back for the party. But she initially refused to do so. Angrily she said to her father, 'All these years I've lived with you. I never disobeyed you. I never stole things from you or ran away from you. I never made you cry. Yet never once did you do anything special for me. But now, the second this tart reappears, you hold a celebration!'

'My daughter,' the father said, 'you are always with me and everything I have is yours and always will be. But we must celebrate and be glad because this sister of yours was dead but now she is alive again. She was lost and now is found. Please come to the party.'

The younger daughter – I want it now!

Sally was rebellious. She was strong-willed, thought she knew best and certainly did not want to be told what to do. Her elder sister was more compliant, happier to fit the mould and never wanting to rock the boat. Their father loved them both equally.

But Sally just knew the grass was greener out there. She was not prepared to let life pass her by. She wanted the good times and she wanted them now. As it didn't seem likely that her father was going to drop dead and leave her an inheritance immediately she would just have to take it. Interestingly, her dad could have stayed in the shop and stopped her but he chose not to. He wanted her to make the right choices but loved her enough to let her choose. That evening he may have deeply regretted doing so, but in his heart of hearts he knew he had to let his child discover for herself some of the harsh realities of life.

Sadly, Sally seemed also unable to confide in her elder sister. Perhaps she seemed too aloof, or looked down on her rebellious little sister. For whatever reason, Sally thought she knew better than anyone and the superficial bright lights and empty promises seduced her to move far away. She didn't want to be found, not because she felt guilty but because she didn't want her fun to end.

It is interesting how money can seem to buy 'friends'. When some years ago I wrote my book about the lottery, one winner said that for the rest of his life he would never know whether people were making friends with him or with his wallet. It is those who stick by you through thick and thin and tell you how it really is who are true friends. Unfortunately for Sally, she had left them behind in her home town.

The cost of sin

Pride is a really damaging emotion. At some stage, probably when the man she believed loved her made her sleep with men for money, Sally should have realized that her dream had become a nightmare and that she should swallow her pride and try to go back home. But she was too afraid of letting her family and friends know she had blown it. Still, she had moments between the unwelcome knocks on the door to start reflecting on what had happened and to come to the inevitable conclusion that it was her fault that she was in this position and that she had made some really bad choices.

Anyone who lives selfishly will end up like Sally, becoming a slave to their selfish desires. The desires of the body can soon take over from the reasoning of the mind, which is why it is often said that someone's rational thought disappears out of the window the second someone starts paying them attention. There are other dangers as well. Loving money and things can also, for example, lead to a gambling addiction. But there is still hope! Anyone can come to their senses.

Jesus never understates sin. In fact he stresses both its cost and its consequences. But he does not believe that sin is an inevitable ongoing part of our humanity. With everything in him he wills for us to turn away and say sorry.

The Father – total forgiveness and restored relationship

Just like Sally, we may well find saying sorry the hardest thing to do, but we will always be so glad when we make up our mind to do so. We may try to build up long explanations or rambling apologies, but it is unnecessary. Every one of us, when in our desperation we turn to God, gets the same reception. In his mercy he accepts us and loves us. We don't understand why because we know that humanly his forgiveness is not justifiable. But we are so grateful that he does this.

This is why the parable could also be called the Parable of the Prodigal Father. Our heavenly Father is 'prodigal' in terms of the lavish, unrestrained and totally undeserved generosity that he pours down on us. When Sally's dad saw her at the train station he did not care about his dignity. This was not about his reputation: it was about his unconditional love. He must have been thinking constantly about what his daughter might have gone through while she had been away. Just one look would have confirmed his worst fears. But perhaps because he could see that Sally had sunk to the very bottom, he knew he had to let her know that she could be fully restored. This is love in abundance. It is extravagant. It feels out of this world – because that's exactly what it is.

When we return to our beloved heavenly Father, the embrace we receive is not just a sign of our forgiveness; it is more a sign of our restored relationship. It is our Father who takes the initiative. We may be trying to stammer out our apologies but he is no longer listening. He is simply too excited that his precious child has come back home. Sally's dad shows everyone present that the relationship is fully restored when he gives her the family heirloom – the ring that had been handed down through the generations. Amazingly this restoration takes place before Sally has had time to prove she is truly sorry – and so it is in our own experience. Simply acknowledging that we are unworthy is what allows God's unconditional love to flow.

It is wonderful to recognize that however far we have wandered away, whatever possessions we have squandered, however immoral the life we've led, our Father is scouring the horizon for us, waiting for us to appear in the distance. Despite our mess he will know us in an instant. He will know the way we look, the way we walk and how we are thinking. His eyes will fill with tears, but this time they will be tears of joy, not the tears of pain he has shed as we have gone down our own treacherous paths. And when we return, there is no questioning, no inquisition 'just to be sure' of our motivation, no standing down, no quarantine period and no condemnation: just the fullness of our Father's love.

The elder daughter – struggling with judgementalism

When we hear a story like this, it's tempting for some of us to wait for Sally's come-uppance. If we think like the Pharisees, who grumbled about the low life that Jesus mixed with, we're likely to take the side of Kate, the elder sister.

I can't speak for you, but it is true to say of myself that although on more occasions than I would like to recount I have been in the place of the younger daughter, as I have 'matured' as a Christian it has become much easier for me to adopt Kate's position. How can someone who has been behaving well go to a party and actually celebrate the return of someone who has behaved like a tramp and sullied the family name? Maybe every time Kate went out people would point at her and whisper about her younger sister. This was so unfair, as Kate believed that she never did anything wrong. And of course the fact that she saw no fault in herself and felt superior to her sister was her greatest fault.

Kate had always known her father's love for her. In fact when her dad got the message from Sally she was the first person he told. But it wasn't enough. Her thinking was dominated by how she had fulfilled her 'duty', and the contrast between that and the unbridled joy of her father could not have been greater.

We, too, can easily become like Kate: self-righteous saints looking down our noses at others who are struggling. We certainly don't believe they should receive the same love as we 'deserve'. If only they had behaved better, worked harder, kept their passions under control, then maybe they would have merited some favour. Like the characters in this story, we all fail our Father – but some of us really struggle to acknowledge it!

Sally's return should have led to a great and universal celebration but led instead to a family crisis. This happens simply because Kate, like us, cannot grasp just how deep this love is.

'How can someone who has done that ever be forgiven?' But God understands us and our failings, and he knows that we *all* fall into this category. He has no list of lesser or greater sins. We all just sin – and we do so repeatedly. However, he will give a kiss to a prodigal who repents and call those who don't 'hypocrites and empty tombs'.

I wonder which of the two sisters you would prefer to have round for a meal! Kate may have been hard-working but she was judgemental, self-righteous and ungrateful. She had been spared all the degradation that her sister had gone through and had been close to her father and so in receipt of his love every day. Yet she probably resented her father's love for her sister and secretly wanted him just to forget about her and concentrate on Kate herself.

By being so selfish, Kate had actually lost relationship with her father too. She just didn't realize it. She is desperately wanted at the party and is the first person to be asked to go, but she refuses because she is not the one in whose honour it is being held.

The need for genuine love and acceptance

It is this arrogance and self-righteousness that is not found in Jesus but sadly is found in many of us. This is why the Father pleads with the Kates of this world. They may be 'good' but they are certainly not attractive. By giving the impression that they are 'good enough' to go to church, they may put off millions who will never go because they think they are not good enough!

We need each other, yet often the single parent, the divorced person, the unemployed, the elderly and especially the homosexual are sidelined in our churches, as those who 'have it all together' enjoy communion one with another. Yet in this parable Sally had to lose all material things before she could find her true inheritance, given by Jesus as a free gift in total love. Kate, on the other hand, was also offered an invitation to the party of unconditional love but had not made up her mind whether to accept it.

Jesus is inviting you to an eternal party in heaven that will be full of sinners who have simply said 'sorry'. Are you going to accept?

10. Lost and Found

Luke 15:1–10

The Pharisees were offended that Jesus not only welcomed people who had led bad lives but even ate with them: this was because they did not understand his love. The good news of Jesus is available to all, but in some ways it is easier to grasp the love and forgiveness on offer when we are painfully aware of our own shortcomings. That is why this story is important – especially for any of us who have ever looked down on others.

An experienced mountaineer took ten cadets on a climb in mid-winter. It was a safe enough climb if you knew the route, but treacherous if you wandered off the slopes.

Coming back down the mountain, he suddenly realized that one cadet was missing. Immediately he stopped and ordered the other nine to stay at the entrance of a nearby cave. Desperately he retraced his steps, fearing that the lost cadet would be dead. Imagine his joy when he heard the faint cries of the young man! He was found on the ground, dirty and defeated by all he had had to endure that day. Looking up thankfully, he whispered, 'I'm so sorry I wandered off. I just wanted to see the view from over there. It looked attractive and didn't seem too far off the track. I realize now how easy it is to be sidetracked and to fall as a result. Thank you so much for coming back to rescue me. I didn't deserve it.' Gently the mountaineer picked the young man up and carried him back to be with the others who had not gone astray.

As soon as he got safely down the mountain, the mountaineer could not wait to meet up with his friends in the local pub.

'What a day I've had!' he cried. 'I lost someone in my charge today and I thought he had gone. But please have a pint with me and let's celebrate, because I've found him. He is safe.'

In exactly the same way there will be more rejoicing in heaven over one sinner who repents than over ninety-nine righteous persons who feel no need to repent.

A young woman is about to go on holiday abroad with a group of friends. The night before, as she packs, she cannot find her passport. Will she not forget about sleep, switch on all the lights and go through every single drawer in the house until she finds it? And when she finds it she calls all her friends who have been anxiously waiting and says, 'Celebrate with me! I've found the passport and will be able to come on holiday with you after all. The drinks are on me tomorrow!'

In the same way, there is rejoicing in the presence of the angels of God over one sinner who repents.

Outrageous grace

I don't know about you, but I feel an almost continuous sense of joy that I know Christ. This may be because I am only too well aware of my own shortcomings. The hurt that I have caused several people in my life could never be put right by myself, and so I would have had a continuous feeling of guilt were it not for Jesus. Yet he has chosen to set me free by taking the punishment that I deserve. This is outrageous grace: undeserved and yet so vitally needed by all of us.

This parable is about the joy of knowing Jesus, but it is also about the supreme importance of the individual to God. Each one of us matters. Each one is loved so much. God wants to carry us gently so that we can be truly rescued from the many things that ensnare us.

Lost or found ... or both?

The story shows how God himself shares in the joy of finding what we are really looking for. But it is also a story of loss. It is about how desperate God is when we are 'lost', when we go astray and don't follow him.

Can we be Christians and still be lost? Many religious people can read these parables and struggle to identify with the lost cadet. They do not see themselves as lost, as they have been christened or been to church occasionally and so couldn't possibly be in that category. Others among us may be the faithful ones who always tithe, fast and pray. They couldn't be referred to here, surely. Or could they?

Those who have made a commitment to Christ are in one sense not lost at all, because they will go to heaven when they die. But if we do not maintain an intimate relationship with God and instead seek out new and temporary thrills we can rapidly lose our direction, just like the cadet on the mountain. The more lost we feel, the more we lose sight of the one true path and therefore the more temptations and choices we seem to have. Our life soon loses all meaning.

Experiencing joy

If we do not know and constantly feel the love of God, we will feel lost and will struggle to experience the joy in our lives that only Christ can bring. If you are not experiencing joy at the moment, just reflect on his great love for you. As an individual. As you are. I would recommend an exercise to do three times a day. Just stand in front of a mirror, take a good look at yourself and repeat out loud, 'I am perfect, blameless and beautiful in God my Father's sight.' Allow yourself to spend time with your Father in heaven. Stop rushing around looking after your family for a few moments and climb on your Daddy's knee and let him hold you, affirm you, encourage you, love you. Let him wipe your tears away. And remember, this is your perfect Dad. You do not have to do things or achieve things before he will love you. He could not love you any more than he does already. Come on – soak it up, and then soak it up some more!

You see, you really are special. Believe this and you will feel joy. Disbelieve and you will feel lost. If we don't believe God can love us, how can we love or even accept ourselves? This low self-esteem causes so much harm and yet many of us Christians suffer from it. We suffer because we have not grasped the sheer joy of understanding that God has found us and rescued us and we couldn't be in a safer or better place than in the arms of our loving Father.

Is fear preventing you from knowing the joy of Christ? Are you worried about death? Do you constantly think you fall short? Or maybe that you are just too insignificant – after all it's 'just me – a disappointment'. Stop concentrating on the times you don't get it right. If we got it right all the time Jesus would never have needed to come to earth! Think instead about the progress you are making, the things you are slowly but gladly overcoming, even if there are many backward steps too.

Walking towards freedom

Think of two people for a moment. One never drinks and looks down on those who do. The other has always drunk too much and has vowed to give it up. He goes for a week and then has a drink. Then he lasts a month without one, then a year. The self-righteous person would say, 'See: he's failed again.' But Jesus would say, 'Just look at the amazing progress he's making. He used to rely on alcohol and now he relies on me. I am so proud of him!' What is more, he would be saying this to the angels, softly speaking our name in love to those closest to him.

For alcohol you can substitute cigarettes, pornography, gambling, lust, greed or one-hundred-and-one other things that we can feel so bad about and which other 'super-Christians' may condemn us for. But it is this group that usually has the greatest problem with joy. Because they see themselves as so godly and Spirit-filled, they believe that they cannot be lost in the first place. They therefore are unable to experience the joy of being found! The joy of experiencing God's grace in the face of all our sin! It is easier for some of us to criticize the sinners around us and end up judgemental and unable to share the pain of those who are hurting. By being like this we are in fact demonstrating just how far away from Jesus we are, and how lost we really are ourselves.

Pursued by God

So here is a litmus test for your faith. Can you believe, having just read these two parables, that God would actively pursue someone who was lost and behaving in a sinful manner and rejoice unconditionally when he was found?

Fortunately God is so much kinder than we are. We write people off. 'There he goes again,' or 'It's only a matter of time before it happens again,' or 'A leopard never changes his spots.' We will give up on people. They're too demanding and take up too much time. 'They'll never learn,' or 'What's the point? He never listens.' But God actively searches for the lost. And at the first sign of the lost actively seeking him he is there rejoicing like crazy.

So hold on to the fact that you have been found. You are free from your guilt and free from fear – even the fear of death. You are going to spend eternity with him. You are perfect, pure, untarnished, and loved beyond belief. And this is how it will be for evermore. I can feel this joy boiling over in me as I write this. Please feel it as well!

11. New Trousers

Luke 5:36–38

No one tears a patch from a new pair of trousers and sews it onto an old one. If you do, you will have torn the new clothes and the patch from the new will look much too bright against the faded material of the old. And no one cooking an omelette would add good eggs to a bad egg that had been cracked open into a pan. If they did that, the bad egg would mix with all the good eggs and the whole meal would end up ruined. You have to start again by putting the new eggs in a clean frying pan.

A changing yet growing faith

For many, change is frightening. This is especially true if you feel reasonably content with your lot and see no reason to change. It is sometimes much easier to reflect on what God was doing in your life ten years ago and bask in that than to face up to what he is wanting to change this instant. We all need to be constantly changing as our Christian faith deepens and we grasp new revelation of what the Lord is saying to us.

We are on a journey and the path is pretty narrow. It goes over hills and round bends that we can't see. There is no point in stopping. Jesus is leading us down the perfect path. We just have to follow him, trusting him even when we are moving into uncharted territory. It may be daunting and at times even frightening, but if we go where we are called the new places will be so rewarding.

Expect the unexpected!

The teaching of these parables demonstrates that there are always new things to learn from God. We simply cannot hear of him and accept him but then stay in the same place. Doing that for too long leads us to stagnate and we can even end up like the bad egg if we stay there indefinitely. By staying the same we run the risk of 'going off' and becoming not only irrelevant but off-putting as well. Just as a pond needs a stream or other fresh water flowing into it to keep it fresh and what lives in it alive, so we need to be always moving forward in the power of the Holy Spirit so that we can continue to impact the lives of those we meet. That's why Jesus challenged the Pharisees about their understanding of God, and he often does the same to us. Just as we think we have grasped what he is like, we see yet another side to him.

Our God is not a God of the past. He doesn't always do things the same way; in fact he often does what we least expect. Jesus mixed with tax collectors and prostitutes as easily as, and perhaps more easily than, he did with the teachers of the law.

It is useful to know of the old ways and we should be grateful for all that God has done through his people in the past. But we should not try to add on bits of the new to the past, as it simply dilutes past achievements and at the same time can ruin the new. Rather we should draw on what has been revealed to Christians during the past two millennia and let this guide us forward.

Jesus cannot simply be 'patched' into our lives and shaped around our beliefs and prejudices. Nor can he be moulded to our future plans or behaviour patterns. He is 'new every morning'. He may always be constant in what he is saying but he will always be finding new ways for us to experience him and show him to others.

Old clothes can be comforting – but they can also be worn out and smelly! Something good that is kept too long and not used when it should be can also rapidly turn from being useful to useless. It can even damage other previously usable items around it.

Looking forward

Are we open to the new workings of the Spirit? This is not to seek change for change's sake, because if we try to do this in our own strength there will be no substance to what we are doing. It will simply mean that a project might be started but not finished, and we will look shallow and foolish. We need to change as and when God gives us a new calling. This can be individually, as a family, or as a church.

Radical change is always difficult and we need to seek wise counsel when it presents itself. We do not want to be deaf to God's calling, but equally we need to test what we think we are hearing with mature Christian leaders to ensure we are on the right lines. It is still acceptable to 'put out a fleece' for a sign of confirmation, just as Gideon did when he wanted to know the will of God. This, in effect, means asking God for an indication which either confirms or denies what we believe to be the right way ahead. I can recall doing so when I quit my well-paid job in the City to work for a small Christian charity. Humanly speaking, I could not perceive that it was right to change, but sound advice and some very clear signals proved that it was. And now I am so glad that I made the change!

The cost – and the reward

Change is frightening because it is all to do with releasing control. It is trusting that we will be better clothed in God than we will be if left to our own devices. To take the story to rather extreme lengths, it is trusting God that the new eggs he has for us are much better than the ones we had already!

Going into new places with God is never easy, but we cannot keep one foot in the old world and one in the new. We must be prepared for some pain and some criticism from others who do not fully understand. It may even be that we pick up some physical or mental scars as a result of the difficult decision to move on with God.

This is an essential part of our walk with God. There is a cost to following Jesus, but there is also a wonderful reward. For part of this life we may have to pick up our cross and carry it, but we can be assured that we will spend eternity wearing a crown of the Kingdom of heaven.

As we move forward, we see both growth and transformation in our lives. We see that just as the old trousers, although comfortable, became threadbare, so our lives need to move ever forward, even though this will involve leaving our comfort zones and adjusting to the new.

We must not compromise our faith and mix the perfect with the less good, never mind the bad. Nor must we ever try to cling to things that have been a comfort to us when we know God is moving us on. God really does have perfect plans for us. Are we ready for the new things he has in store for us?

12. Justice Done

Luke 18:1–8

Here is another story to encourage you always to pray and not give up.

In a certain town there was a solicitor who didn't really care about justice or his clients. He just wanted to make as much money as he possibly could. One of his clients was a single mother who was owed child support by her ex-husband. The solicitor had no interest in the case, since he made no money out of it, but she used to pester him endlessly because her needs were so great. 'All I want is justice,' she would often say. 'I only want what is due to me.'

For some time he kept trying to put her off in the hope that she might go away or try to deal with the Child Support Agency herself. But finally he realized she was not going to give up, so he said to himself, 'Even though I couldn't care less about her case and I will make no money out of it, I am going to resolve this case because this woman is beginning to wear me down. I will ensure she gets justice before her constant pleas give me a breakdown. She has become a pain in the neck!'

Now just look at what the selfish solicitor said! How much more, then, will our just God ensure that his children, who cry out to him day and night, are well looked after and see their prayers answered? Do you think he would ever say to them, 'I'm too busy,' or 'You're not a priority to me'? Of course not: he is always eager to answer our prayers. He will see to it that they get justice and quickly. When Jesus returns, however, will he find this degree of faith on earth?

Fair treatment

In Jesus' time there were various groups, including widows, who were treated really shabbily and were often denied justice. You would think that in today's society this was a thing of the past, but, sitting as a magistrate, I can assure you that some groups still struggle to be treated fairly. Maybe they are written off as trouble-makers or as people who have brought things on themselves. Because of their vulnerabilities, be they social, cultural or language-related, they are often deprived of the very basics of life. Yet these are the very ones who need help the most! Many will despair and give up, just as the solicitor in this case hoped the single mother would do, but there will be a few who are brave enough to stand up for themselves and eventually see justice done.

The lazy solicitor would have acted much more quickly if he had been paid. He might have done things a lot faster if he had been dealing with a twenty-stone skinhead who looked as though he ate skinny solicitors for breakfast! But the only recourse for the single mum was to nag him into action. He did not fear her, but the constant drip, drip effect eventually found its mark. He would do what he could for her.

In our interests

The point of the story, of course, is to contrast the solicitor with God. The former only acted out of self-interest; God only acts in our best interest. The solicitor eventually acted, but reluctantly and only because he had been forced into it: our loving Father delights in hearing from us and granting us the desires of our heart, as long as they are in our best interests and not harmful to others. The single mother only asked for what was fair for herself and her family, and our prayers need to mirror that.

Sometimes we give up all too easily. We want instant answers and if they don't come we assume God isn't listening. But he may well be testing us to see just how serious our request is, or he might be putting things into place that will give us an answer way beyond our wildest dreams. So, if something is really important to us let's keep on praying!

13. Me, Me, Me

Luke 12:16–21

Nearly everybody these days wants more and more things for themselves, and what is more, they want them yesterday. As Christians, we might pray to God for even more things we don't really need. It is so easy for us to be greedy and act as if we believe that what we have makes us what we truly are. We all need to grasp the words of Jesus that a person's life does not consist in the abundance of their possessions. So take a look at this story.

A rich industrialist had had an excellent year and got an enormous bonus. He thought to himself, 'Just how am *I* going to spend this? *I* work so hard that *I* am perfectly justified in spending this on *myself*.'

Then he thought, '*I* know what *I* will do. *I* will buy another large house in the country just in case *I* ever get a day off. *I* will furnish it with expensive ornaments and the most extravagant furnishings *I* can buy. *I* will purchase a new top-of-the-range convertible with *my* own personalized number-plate. *I* could even afford a private jet. This would be very useful because *I* am such an important person and it would help *me* to get around all *my* businesses quicker. Then *I* will be able to look around and say to *myself*, "Look at what *I* have achieved." *I* have got so much here, *I* really will be able to enjoy *myself* in the years ahead. One day, *I* keep promising *myself*, *I* will take life easy. *I* will drink, eat and be merry.'

But the man lived like a fool. He lived just for himself. He lived as if this life would go on for ever. But that night he died. So who now is going to get all the things he had so selfishly stored up for his future use?

The message of this story is clear. This is how it is going to be for everyone who hoards things for himself and ignores God's teaching and the desperate needs of others.

While many people struggle through life barely managing to survive, others seem to coast along effortlessly. To them life is a doddle; everything smells of roses, everything they touch seems to turn to gold. Life will always be like this. They haven't a care in the world. Then they die.

Intolerable gaps between us and them

How do you feel when you read that the three hundred richest people in the world have more accumulated wealth than the poorest 50 per cent of the entire world's population? Or even worse, that the three richest people in the world have more wealth than the forty-eight poorest countries? Is this right? But for the grace of God it could be you and I starving in one of those forty-eight countries, desperately looking to our brothers and sisters in Christ in the prosperous countries such as the UK to do something about it. We need to be aware of these facts and then we need to do something positive about it. Not paying lip service to this but living as simply as we can and giving as generously and as often as we can. This is not communism. This is unconditional love in action.

More does not mean better

Jesus strongly disapproves of all actions that have underlying selfish motives. He also teaches that just having more will never in itself truly satisfy. Just because we have more money it does not mean that our lives will be any better. In fact there is ample evidence to suggest that really rich people live increasingly isolated and unfulfilled lives. The more possessions we have, the more time, money and effort it takes to maintain them. So both God and others get squeezed out. After all, if we started really applying God's teaching or caring about the poor we might have to get rid of the very things we covet so much. So we keep on accumulating until one day, when we are still blissfully unaware, possessions start possessing us! In this particular parable the rich man can only talk to himself about what he feels he has achieved. Nobody else is pleased or interested. In fact he is likely to have many enemies, as he seems not to have shared his good fortune with anyone else.

Selfishness leads to loneliness

No one else is mentioned in this story. Nobody else shares his life, his pleasures. Wealth brings resentment and increasing isolation – though often this is caused directly by the rich themselves. The larger the house you have, the bigger the gates; the taller the fences, the greater the security. Suddenly you have done so well for yourself that you have created your own expensive prison.

But living without thinking about the needs of others can only lead to a warped perspective on life. So the rich man's thinking and actions usually start and stop with him. He dares not look beyond himself. He needs to know just how well he is doing now. Does he have more than yesterday? He worries that things may go wrong tomorrow, so he concentrates on the here and now. He certainly never thinks beyond this world.

Jesus never directly condemned money or wealth, but he was only too well aware of how damaging the love of money is. He constantly warned about the negative impact that too much more or too many things can have in our lives. Often he spoke about this with real pity because he knows more than anyone the cost of surrendering things for the sake of others. This is why his non-materialistic words so strongly challenge our comfort zones and convict us if we, as committed Christians, try to ignore his teaching.

Surrender everything

Jesus tells us that real life is not measured by possessions. When Christians in the developed countries genuinely put others' needs before their never-ending wants we might even get revival! We can have a big bank balance, but if we ignore God and others we are poor, not rich. We are behaving in a foolish and shortsighted manner. It could be that by preparing for our everyday comfort we have damaged our place in eternity. It was Jesus who said in Luke 14:33, 'Any of you who does not give up everything he has cannot be my disciple.' You don't have to have been to Bible College to understand this verse!

This may sound daunting but it is exceptionally good news! By grasping this truth and becoming generous to others we are storing up treasures in heaven that will never fade. Things on earth are superficial and temporary, yet the desire for them can steer us away from what is really important – relationship with God and with others.

We are rich already

In this story the man is already rich before he gets the bonus. In fact, he has so much he just doesn't know what to do with it all. He is not accused of any dishonesty and is looking forward to a day when he might retire and have the time to enjoy the money he is spending on himself. You have to question, however, given that the man was putting all his trust in his wealth, whether he would ever feel secure enough to start spending it.

Look outwards and upwards!

In today's society this 'success story' would be regarded as a key player. He would appear regularly in the media and at conferences. He would be a well-known name. Jesus called him a fool – not because of his success but because of his wrong priorities. As Christians we are called to be in the world but not of it, not to be so absorbed by our possessions that they and we become one and the same. So this story is a clear warning to us.

Jesus is telling us to stop concentrating on the things on earth because they are trivial. He pleads with us not to be so focused on ourselves. Look again at the parable. It's all 'I', 'myself' and 'my'. Surely this man has not achieved all this by himself. Where is the mention of his workers, his suppliers or his customers? How about others who have been involved in his life – his parents, teachers, trainers? Where is God in his thinking? The answer sadly is that the rich fool brings no one else into the equation. He believes it is his talent alone that has enabled him to be so 'successful' and so he concentrates purely on 'self' – the rudest four-letter word in the English language.

The dangers of greed

But despite the fact that he was already incredibly wealthy he still wanted more. He thought that maybe one day there would be enough, but he seems to have kept raising this figure, with the result that he would never be able to reach it. This is a valuable lesson to all of us. At the end of the day this constantly wanting more will not work. There will never be enough. Get a great house and you'll want to furnish it nicely. Then you might 'need' a new car, an expensive holiday, a holiday home, a yacht, a jet. How about two of each, or three, or four? Do you think this is fanciful? Do you believe that many of us ask, 'When is enough, enough?' Do we naturally stop when we get to a certain size of house and a reasonable holiday, or each year does it have to be just that little bit better than the one before?

I repeat: this will never work. Only recently I read in the newspapers of a lottery winner who was declared bankrupt. At one stage, in an effort to find happiness he had owned nineteen cars at the same time. The man who craves wealth is like a man who drinks seawater. The more he has, the greedier and more desperate he becomes for more, until he dies.

Earth is just our temporary resting place

The world is a bridge. The wise man will pass over it but will not build his house upon it. We all need to remind ourselves constantly that our time on earth is but a stepping-stone to the next world that awaits us. This is the reason why we are here in the first place. But we all continue disastrously to suffer stress, debt and break-downs in the idle pursuit of temporary pleasures. The tragedy of this story is that the impending death of the rich man is only reminding us of something that we already know: his soul is already dead. By concentrating on money and things rather than God and people we are dying as we live. Knowing God and loving and being loved by others is real treasure. We need to remember that the instant that death occurs, the narrow gap between ourselves and our possessions becomes an unbridgeable chasm.

Even as Christians we can measure success by title, wealth or house. People even seek to express their own importance and immortality by having a personalized number plate on their car! Yet the more we have, the more anxious and dissatisfied we become. Everything needs to be bigger, newer and certainly better than our neighbours'! It is so easy to blame our materialistic culture, but if we behave selfishly it is our own responsibility.

Do you have enough?

In our world, our country, our town and our church there will be a wide range of circumstances. You may be on benefits, struggling to survive week in, week out, in which case this story is not for you. But many of us already have more than enough. We will be buying things we don't need, often on credit with money we don't have, in order to try to impress people we don't even like! We will 'need' to be driving the 'right' car and be wearing the trendiest (and most expensive) label. We will want to be seeing a constantly increasing standard of living. After all, this is our right. If this is what is driving us on we need to be careful. With the mis-selling of personal pensions and endowments in recent years, many of us are facing normal retirement age with nothing like enough savings. So we will need to be prepared for a much lower standard of living or keep on working well past retirement age. It will not be long in any event before this is such a crisis that the Government will increase the retirement age to seventy. You have been warned!

At the moment we still see increasing standards of living as a right. Yet in the past fifteen years alone, the gap between the richest 10 per cent of the world's population (which includes nearly all of us in the UK) and the poorest 10 per cent has doubled. In a small way this is to do with government and corporate policies. In a much bigger way it is to do with greed.

The rich industrialist ignored his neighbours. He had not learnt that selfishness can never bring true enjoyment. J.M. Barrie summed it up by saying, 'Those who bring sunshine into the lives of others cannot keep it from their own.' It is our Lord who is dying of starvation in Ethiopia, of Aids in Africa, of debt in Britain. There but for God's grace could be you and I as well.

Selfishness makes us ignore others

The rich man also forgot time. When we die, only our inward treasure goes with us. Consider for a moment: have we made the right choice between God's eternal blessings and temporary earthly treasure? God's timing is not our own. It is so easy to make assumptions about the future and expect to sort things out later, but death puts a full stop to that. If we concentrate only on ourselves we will have little or nothing to take with us. Nor will we have the glorious welcome from those who have entered heaven before us and are so glad to see us there.

Ultimately the rich fool forgot the very God who had created him. The most important factor in his life had been ignored. Real treasure is loving others, but it especially has to do with welcoming Jesus as our Lord and Saviour, because he has done everything for us.

So to conclude this story, we become rich by letting go and by giving generously. In today's consumer society it is easy to be like the rich man and forget that a person is what they are, not what they have. Death will not take away kindnesses or fond memories. All of us need to remember that we cannot take material things with us. There are no pockets in a shroud. So Jesus tells us that the supreme aim in life is to develop a generous character, because this will find favour with God and our neighbours. If we pursue this, we too will benefit greatly as we become more like the most generous person ever – our beloved Jesus.

14. The Big Issue

Luke 16:19–31

There was a rich young man who worked in the City. He always wore the latest fashions and lived in absolute luxury every day. Outside his office was a poor man, Dave, who tried to earn a living by selling copies of the *Big Issue*. He was very poor and his only friend seemed to be his dog, which would sit with him and keep him warm on cold winter days.

One day the *Big Issue* seller died and found himself in the luxury of heaven. The rich man also died and had an elaborate funeral. In hell, where he was in torment, he looked up and saw God far away with the *Big Issue* seller by his side. So he called out, 'Father God, have pity on me and send that chap to dip the tip of his finger in water and cool my tongue, because I am in agony down here.'

But God replied, 'Son, remember that in your lifetime you received your good things, while this poor young man had next to nothing. But now Dave is comforted here and you are in endless agony. And beside all this, there is a great chasm between us that cannot be crossed one way or the other.'

The rich man replied, 'If this is true then please, God, send someone to my father's house on earth, because I have a large family and none of them believes this to be true. Let somebody warn them so at least they too will not have to enter this place of endless torment.'

God replied, 'But my Son died for them. It is also written in the Bible. They need to pay heed to all the signs that are already so clearly spelled out.'

'That's no good,' the rich man replied. 'They think like I used to do, that this is all a load of rubbish. But now I know it's true. If you were only to send someone from the dead or give some other miraculous sign, I am sure they would radically alter their views.'

But God said to him, 'If they will not believe the evidence that is all around them, if they will not even believe the words of my beloved Son Jesus, they will never be convinced – even if someone was raised from the dead they would try to explain it away!'

It is not ours!

The condemnation of greatly differing levels of wealth is one of the most regularly repeated messages of Jesus' ministry. The gaps in our world between rich and poor are obscenely large, so this teaching needs ramming home to comfortable decadent Christians in the west as never before. This is because this gap between rich and poor is not condemned in our churches: it is mirrored in them. We can criticize the desperate single mum buying a lottery ticket, but we see nothing wrong in spending thousands on private health care for ourselves. (After all, there is nothing wrong with wanting the best for ourselves, is there?)

This story is, however, not a new message just for today's materialistic society. We all tend to want to keep things for ourselves. Church fathers have tried through the ages to address the issue. Augustine said, 'To succour the needy is justice' and Ambrose said, 'You are not giving the poor person the gift of a part of what is yours. You are returning something to him which is really his.' Chrysostom said, 'Do not say, "I am spending what is mine." It is not actually yours. It is someone else's.' Basil said, 'It is the hungry one's bread you keep, the needy one's money you have hoarded,' and Jerome said, 'All riches originally derive from injustice.'

Are you beginning to get the picture? Every time I read this parable I feel very uneasy. In fact, I need to share something with you. As I started to work on this parable, I was all ready to lambaste the rich young man for his uncaring nature when a little voice inside my head pointed out to me that I was no different. What was I doing personally to improve the lot of people like Dave? As a result of this I went through a period when I was unable to write a word. It lasted over three months. So if you ever feel there is a finger pointing at you, I can assure you that there are at least three pointing at me.

We need to do something

We do need to remember, however, that Jesus repeatedly criticized unfeeling wealth and encouraged the un-complaining poor. He spoke out against those who had been blessed with so much yet could turn their backs on those with little or nothing. We of course do not want to see ourselves like that. We're not Pharisees. We can read about the feasts that kings held in castles in the Middle Ages while their people outside were starving, and we rightly feel disgusted. But in one thousand years' time will people look at our society, notice the huge gaps between rich and poor and wonder how we even dared to call ourselves Christians? Or to bring it back to today, how many people struggling to survive in the Third World would look at us in the UK and not begin to wonder how we could so selfishly strive for even more when our brothers and sisters are literally starving to death? Yet one of the fastest growing aspects of Christianity in the wealthy west is the obscenity of the 'prosperity gospel', according to which as 'King's kids' we should just think of ourselves and give to God because he is some form of glorified slot machine in the sky that will pay out tenfold the money we give him. What an awful motivation: it is just like claiming we buy lottery tickets to give to charity when only 7 per cent actually goes to this. Yet we can be like the prosperity followers and want more for ourselves now. What an appalling charade!

We need to do things now

This story says that though people let the poor down, God never will. Everyone is special to him and is known by name. We might expect to find that it is the rich young man who is identified in the story by name, not the *Big Issue* seller. After all, at our conferences the successful man would be on the platform while the *Big Issue* seller would be kept to one side, out of sight. But the high and mighty on earth are not of greater importance to God than the poor and lowly.

The parable shows something we are very good at forgetting: that the chasms seen on earth between the ways different people live are reflected in eternity. On earth we can change things – the rich can narrow the gap between themselves and the poor whenever they choose – but by the time we die it is too late to change things. In the story the rich young man was clothed in all the latest 'designer labels'. He no doubt travelled first class from his large country house and didn't even notice the guy selling the *Big Issue* outside his office. He would never have purchased a copy or struck up a conversation with him. They could even both be Christians, but if no communication takes place between them how will one understand the other?

What we can 'afford' is irrelevant

The designer labels and the personal number plates shout out today about how we've got it all together. We can boast about our wealth and success through our houses and holidays. It is important to stress here that the rich man in the story lived in absolute luxury *every* day. All of us like to eat good food and to be entertained: God knows this and will often pour out these blessings on us. But to behave like this as if it is the norm rather than a special treat shows selfishness, particularly when there is so much real need in our world. In fact the rich man is criticized not so much for his wastefulness as for his lack of concern for others. He just enjoyed living like that. He could 'afford' to do so, so why should he think about anyone else?

Interestingly, John Wesley is reported to have said that 'afford' was the word he hated most in the English language. He claimed it was an attempt by people to justify the unjustifiable and in any event, as it is God's money, it is not ours to afford in the first place! Certainly it should never be used as a justification for the way we live.

What needs to hit home to us even more is the fact that this story never condemns the rich man as a rogue or a cheat. There is no mention of dishonesty or unscrupulous behaviour. The fact that Dave was able to sell his magazine outside the office implies that the rich man might even have thought that he was demonstrating kindness. After all, there were probably many offices that had refused to let him stand outside.

Really helping the poor

But, importantly, the rich man did nothing to help Dave to improve his situation. By allowing the status quo to continue ('the rich man in his castle, the poor man at his gate') he was in fact acquiescing in the injustice. Dave just needed to get through the day. He wasn't looking for a continuous improvement; he just wanted to survive.

Are we like this rich man? It is easy for our 'love' and 'concern' to be in reality so shallow that they can cause outrage. We see people as we pass them every day, but do they register as people like Dave with real practical needs that we could address with minimal cost and effort? We are far more likely to be judgemental about people like the *Big Issue* seller ('I bet he spends all his money on drink or drugs') than to be moved by his plight.

Reacting to the needs of others

It is so easy to think that these things are nothing to do with us. It's just the way life is. It is not the fact that the young man was rich that is a problem – because that is an enormous opportunity. It is the fact that he was selfish. In times gone by he would probably have known how good it felt to be loving and compassionate, but the lure of riches had blinded him to a truth he once would have known. People born into poverty have no choice. Those born into relative wealth do. It is much easier to covet what someone else has than it is to think, 'I am so blessed; there but for the grace of God go I.' Personal greed can rapidly remove the potential for good.

True love is about ongoing commitment. Buying a copy of the *Big Issue* would have been a start, a smile just as important. But giving cannot be superficial or occasional. Christians must not accept the gulf between the rich and the poor, between the powerful and the powerless. I am so good at 'justifying' my position and therefore explaining away where other people are at – as if this is somehow meant to be. ('It must be their fault.')

But the story doesn't tell us there is anything good or bad about Dave. He is in fact just poor. This is important, otherwise we rich could justify our position by saying that if we had realized that underneath he really was a good man we would have helped him. This story is just about the divide between rich and poor. It is also about the divide between this world and the next, and between heaven and hell.

Are we ready for heaven?

In the parable the death of the men immediately brings a reversal of roles. The rich man finds himself in hell and realizes the true state of events when he 'looks up' and sees Dave in heaven. ('That chap looks vaguely familiar. Isn't he that down-and-out that used to try and sell things outside my office? What on earth is he doing up there with God?') It is a startling role reversal, because now Dave is rich in respect and companionship whereas the rich man, who would have been used to many people doing things for him, has no one even to get him a drink of water.

The rich man instantly recognized that what he had previously thought of as good on earth was in fact trivial and inconsequential in the light of eternity. Worse still, he realized that death was the finishing line in only one respect – that there was no way of bridging the gap between heaven and hell. Choices on earth clearly determine where eternity will be spent.

But this chasm has in fact been created not by God but by humankind itself. The more we ignore the needs of others, the more selfish we become. In behaving like this we are actually digging our own chasm. Every selfish action makes it deeper and that much harder to fill. God wants our compassion to direct our wealth. Instead, we use money to drown our caring nature.

It is interesting that in the story the rich man still sees Dave as someone who should be at his beck and call ('Send him to ... cool my tongue'). But it is too late, because even if Dave had wanted to help he could not do so.

Looking forward

It is fascinating to see in this parable that recognition and memory will exist when we die. What a great joy to be spending eternity with people we love! To see that little acts of kindness on earth will lead to eternal happiness. What a welcome we will receive from those we have led to Christ!

One of the main points of the parable is that if somebody is prepared to be ruthless to get something, they will pay the price for it. The rich young man had chosen earthly things; now he would be paying the price for eternity. In today's society we seem to believe that everything of value has to be purchased. Yet the most important gifts – eternal life and peace of mind – are free gifts given by God should we decide to surrender our lives to him and choose them. Eternity brings compensation and reward for how we live on earth, but it can also bring eternal retribution and a separation from God that cannot be changed. If we follow God fervently, we can rest assured that one day we will be with him in heaven.

Stop looking for sensationalism

Returning to the parable, we see the rich young man starting to think of others at long last as he asks for a sign to be sent to his family. If only they knew for certain about this they would change their ways. The problem with this, of course, is that it would lead to salvation by deeds, however miraculously performed, rather than by faith. Their motive would be fear rather than trust and hope.

Doing God's will

We are still really good at looking for amazing signs and wonders and miraculous healings to bolster our shaky faith. Yet we have the Holy Spirit living within us, prompting and gently guiding us. No 'Dave' should leave me unmoved or unprepared to do anything about him or her. After all, it was not any evil action on the part of the rich man that sent him to prison; it was his sheer inaction that sent him to hell. By doing the best you can to help meet need when you see it, you are demonstrating God's love in action.

To conclude, this story illustrates how important our actions on earth are. Money hoarded for selfish pleasure will eventually lead to disaster; shared with the needy it will bring eternal blessings. Wealth can separate us from others and it can distance us from God. But it will be us moving away from him, not the other way round.

This is not a story to condemn but it is a challenge and a not-so-gentle warning because it talks about the biggest issue we will ever face. Jesus says to us in effect, 'I love you so much. Please join with me and show the love I have for others by meeting their needs. I promise you that you will never regret it!'

God is asking us to partner with him. What a motivation to put others' needs before our wants!

15. Banking on Wealth

Luke 18:18–30

A banker was praying. He had been a Christian for as long as he could remember and always attended church on Sundays. He had a quiet time every day; he tithed, and on special occasions he even fasted. But he had been troubled for some time, so he plucked up courage and asked Jesus, 'What must I do to fully receive eternal life?'

As he listened in silence he heard a still, small voice: 'You know my commandments – do not kill, commit adultery, steal or lie. Have you obeyed them?'

'I have kept all these commandments since I was a child,' the banker replied.

'There is one thing I need to ask you to do, though,' said Jesus. 'Where do you place your security? In worldly terms you are so rich. Why not show that you trust me by selling everything you have and giving the proceeds to the poor? Then you will be storing up treasures you can never lose – treasures in heaven.'

The banker felt as though he'd been shot. Surely he wasn't meant to do this. Surrender all the money he'd worked hard to acquire? Ask his family to adjust to a simpler lifestyle, a smaller house and an older car? For the sake of the poor? Now this was something he really would need to think about. He wasn't sure whether he wanted to pay the cost of following Jesus that closely.

As God watches us wrestling with these issues, he must reflect on how hard it is for wealthy people to really surrender everything to him. He must be sad as he thinks of how many people in the affluent countries stopped truly worshipping him because they were too committed to possessions. He sympathizes with them but wishes they would grasp that those who take that difficult step will never regret it. After all, they would get so many thanks on earth, as well as storing up eternal treasures.

We have so much

In worldly terms we are all rich. If there were only one hundred people alive in the world today, the average person in the United Kingdom would be the ninth richest. Sadly, many of us in the UK, and many Christians in the west, are obsessed by material things, yet often feel dissatisfied and empty. We all want happiness, security and peace of mind. We might believe that these things can be purchased. That if only we had a little more we would be fully satisfied. And as a rich person, we may be used to getting our own way and even believing that this is as it should be. But we cannot use our resources to manipulate God and we should not try to use them to manipulate other people.

Good 'works' don't work!

We may feel insecure about our future, and even as a Christian it is all too easy to try to think of the 'good works' we have done as if somehow this is going to give us bonus points and win us favour with God. Or to put it another way, all we need to do is find the right formula and we will somehow build up credit points with God. Perhaps he'll look at the good things and ignore the bad. Or at the very least see that there is a surplus on the positive side.

It is as if we think we can win our way into heaven. Surely this negates the very point of why Jesus had to come for us: that since God hates sin and we are all sinners, Jesus had to take our sin to make us spotlessly clean.

It is like being on top of a burning building, with another building forty feet away. It makes no difference whether we can jump five feet or twenty-five feet. The end result will be the same. What we need is to be rescued from on high.

As Christians we are always trying to find the right equation and thinking that then somehow all will be well. We need to remember that the only formula that works is this:

$$Jesus + nothing = salvation$$

It is incredibly arrogant of us to think that somehow we can win our way into God's good books. Whatever we do, God cannot love us any more, and whenever we fail he will not love us any less. In fact God loves us so much and our place in heaven is so important to him that he sent his only Son to earth so that we could spend eternity with him. Doesn't it amaze you to think that God was prepared to let his only Son suffer to such an extent on earth for you and me?

True security

We also need to remember that much about Christian lifestyle relates to how we treat our neighbour. All the points mentioned in this story refer to how we interact with our fellow human beings. It is to do with true relationship. It is to see their needs as being at least as important as our own.

When the chips are down, where is our security? Many people try to find security in a house. Maybe then house prices fall, interest rates rise or we lose our job. Suddenly security has turned into anxiety! Our security is to be found only in the arms of our beloved Jesus, and we need to hear his words and look at his priorities so that we can attempt to mirror them in our own lives.

Let me issue a stark challenge: 'How can we say that we are loving our neighbours as ourselves when fellow-believers are dying of hunger or struggling to make ends meet and yet we stuff our houses full of things – none of which we sell and release to them?' Before you throw things at me, these are reportedly the words of Jesus as he tells this parable in the Gospel to the Hebrews (Apocrypha).

We can keep the commandments in a legal sense but at the same time fail to live them out spiritually and in love. The more righteous we are about obeying the rules, the harder it is to see that we are sinners, that we are selfish. It is hard to give everything away. This is especially true today, when society seems to value us according to what we own. What we have seems more important than who we are. But Jesus laid everything down for each one of us.

What things do to us

Possessions encumber us. They weigh us down. The more we have, the more time, money and effort it takes to look after them and so the less time and money and effort we have for God and others. If we hold possessions strictly for our own pleasure God will ask us to give them away. If we are using them to help others we become good stewards of them, and they change from a millstone to a blessing.

Eternal life cannot be purchased with money; it has already been paid for by the blood of Jesus. Not everything of value has a price tag on it. Rich people may be able to buy many things on earth, but they will never be able to buy themselves into heaven.

Do we love some or all of our possessions more than we love other people? If we do, sadly I have to say that we are rejecting Jesus. It's by putting others first that we show we have truly grasped what Jesus has done for us: we need to remember the promise Jesus gives to each of us, that whoever gives up everything to follow him will receive a much greater reward.

The dangers of having money

Riches are dangerous:

- They encourage a false sense of security. You think that if trouble strikes you can buy your way out of it.
- They imply that everything can be bought. Not just things but happiness as well. We think they provide us with some form of independence. They may in fact take away our necessary dependence on God.

- They make us selfish. We always want more. Once we have enjoyed a little luxury we fear we may lose it. So the richer we become, the more we hoard rather than becoming increasingly generous with God's provision. We forget that 'we lose what we gain and gain what we give away'.
- They are tied to earth. If our treasures are tied to earth we are focusing on the trivial and insignificant, because time here is but a blink of an eye compared with the time we will spend in heaven. William Wilberforce said, 'When Christians stop concentrating on the next life they become totally ineffective in this one.'

But don't give up hope! Let God break through. Zacchaeus, Joseph of Arimathea and Nicodemus were some of the wealthiest men around but they chose Jesus. It is not that those who have riches are automatically shut out. It is that they often close the door themselves. So having money is not a sin but it is a real danger.

This story is intended not to condemn but to warn. All of us are rich by worldly and historical standards. We are all to some degree influenced by advertising and our culture. We need to pray about the money and things God has given us. He loves us and wants to give us many blessings. Sometimes we can get these by giving rather than receiving. By putting him first, even we rich can pass through the eye of a needle and receive his never-ending love, grace and forgiveness.

Now those are true riches!

16. Two Masters

Luke 16:1–15

There was a large debt-collection agency that employed people to ensure that all money owed was paid back in full. It came to their attention that one of their managers was not applying these principles ruthlessly enough for their liking. So they called him in and asked him, 'What is this we hear about you? We gather you have not been collecting all the money that is due to us. Please have all your books ready for an audit next week, because if what we hear proves to be correct we will have no alternative but to fire you.'

The manager said to himself, 'What shall I do now? Once they see the books I'm bound to lose my job. I'm too old to get another job and yet I don't want to beg or go on the dole.' He thought for a while and then said, 'I know what I'll do so that when I lose my job here, people will still like me and help me in any way they can.'

So he called each of the debtors and told them to come to his office. He asked the first, 'How much does the statement say you owe this company?'

'£800,' he replied.

The manager told him, 'I've amended the figure. Here is a new bill. Look at the bottom line. It's for £400. Pay that amount and as far as I am concerned you've nothing left to pay.'

Then he asked the second, 'And how much do you owe?'

'£1,000,' he replied.

'I've changed your figure. The amount you owe is now £600.'

The manager did this to all who came when he summoned them.

When the auditors of the company looked at the books and saw what he had done, they felt a grudging admiration for him because he had acted shrewdly.

Worldly people can be much wiser in dealing with their fellow men than believers are. It is important that you use worldly wealth to gain friends for yourself, so that when it is gone you will be welcomed into heaven by many people who love and admire you.

Whoever proves that they are trustworthy in handling small amounts of money by using it God's way can also then be trusted with much, but whoever is dishonest or selfish with little will be the same with larger amounts. Therefore, if you have not been trustworthy in the way you handle money on earth, how can you expect to enjoy the riches of truly knowing God in heaven? If you cannot be trusted with someone else's property, how can you expect to be given things for yourself?

No one can serve two different masters at the same time: you will end up loving one and hating the other, or devoting your time to one and failing to serve the other properly. It's impossible to follow God and also follow money.

Many religious people who are lovers of money can hear this but choose to ignore the teaching. Jesus says to them, 'You are the ones who justify yourselves before men, but God knows your hearts. What you find worthy on earth – money, possessions, status and power – is actually hated by God and will have no place in heaven.'

A difficult tale

This is a difficult parable to interpret, especially as at one level it seems to be endorsing dishonesty. One explanation could be that the manager realized he had not been using all means possible to get everything owed to the company paid promptly, and that as soon as the company found out, he would not only lose his job but face other consequences too. No other company would employ him once they heard how he had been behaving, but even worse would be the strong possibility that the company might decide to take him to court. He could therefore have reasoned that the best thing to do would be to involve the debtors by making them accomplices, which they became as soon as they agreed to accept lower bills than they knew they should have had. They certainly would not go to court to testify against him. The directors might themselves have acted this ruthlessly if it was a matter of protecting the company's best interests, and therefore grudgingly congratulated the manager on his thinking.

Another possibility is that the manager would be on some sort of commission scheme. Many people in this position have a low basic income and rely on the commission they receive on sales or, in this case, the income received from the debtors. These sums are added to the bills or allowed for in the rate of interest that is charged. So what the manager could have decided is that he would forgo much of the money due to him but ensure that enough was paid to ensure the company got back what it was due.

Planning ahead

In any event, the parable is not endorsing dishonesty, nor is Jesus saying that this is a role model for all Christians to follow! What Jesus is doing is not commending the morality of what the manager has done; but rather commending the common sense that he uses once he is called to account. In order to get ahead on earth and have people think well of him, the manager acted more sensibly than many good people do as they try to 'work' their way into heaven.

Take a look for a moment. The manager stopped and worked through his various options. He dismissed those that were unsuitable for his purposes. He assessed the crisis and saw the best way forward. Then he didn't just think or talk about it, he put the plan into action. He was single-minded about his aims and objectives. He knew where he wanted to go and he did all that he could to get there. But he did so in a way that also benefited others. He recognized the struggle that the debtors were going through and was prepared to do what he could to help them cope too. He would forgo some of his income to help them survive. By helping others he was in fact helping himself.

Where is your bottom line?

Jesus tells us (Matthew 10:16) to be 'wise as serpents and innocent as doves' (RSV). As Christians, we are much better at the latter than we are at the former! But what Jesus is saying here is that serpents or snakes plan their days. They know when to rest and when and where to hunt. They plan the best location and they choose their prey carefully. If things weren't planned this way they would simply starve and die. They also have an escape route prepared in case a crisis suddenly faces them.

Jesus is asking us this: when disaster strikes, when a reverse hits us, do we have a strong enough faith to work through it? Is our faith deep enough to cope with the reverses that we may face or are we just 'fair weather' Christians?

Being a Christian does not make us a doormat. We do have opinions and sometimes it is important that they are expressed very forcibly. The key question here is, 'What is the motivation of what we are saying?' If it is to promote self or our particular group at the expense of another, the motivation is wrong and we should remain quiet. If, however, our aim is to expose injustice or suffering elsewhere, we need to be taking strong action.

It is this tension between being 'wise as serpents and innocent as doves' that can make it difficult for many of us to know what to do, so when in doubt we tend to do nothing. Shrewd forward planning is wise and sensible, but often people prefer to wait to be 'led by the Spirit'. Of course, everything we do needs to be covered in prayer and we need to give God time to answer, but many of us struggle to take action over matters that could be considered 'shrewd'.

This is sadly why the church often struggles to fulfil the very things that God has called it to do. Lack of planning and amateurish and half-hearted efforts will lead to failure, and so they should. We are serving a God of excellence and we need to be showing this to a world of very mixed standards. A company selling biscuits would put a major effort into ensuring the success of a new product. A church might try to promote Jesus, the greatest gift any man or woman can ever know, but do it badly or even give up before anything is achieved. Planning and commitment are essential and need to go hand in hand with love and compassion.

In the parable the manager was still trying to save his own skin by bringing people on side. The debtors were equally as keen to feather their own nest by having their debts cancelled. If Christians were this committed to their faith, we would have revival in this land. We can spend hours making our homes, cars, gardens and even our bodies look perfect and only occasionally remember our Lord Jesus, who makes us totally perfect in front of Father God for all eternity.

Obstacles to shrewdness we must overcome

It is easy for many things to get in the way of our being wise planners. 'Are we sure we have heard from God? And in any event we don't really know how to plan.' So doubt and lack of confidence can cripple us before we start. So can low self-esteem or simple weariness, as we think, 'We can't make a difference' or 'We've tried before and no one listened to us.' Then there may be the different plans of others who present them more forcibly than we can. We may struggle with the courage to speak ('Surely God isn't speaking through me?') or simply not want to be involved because what is being proposed involves change.

Despite these obstacles, we must do all we can to play our part and work in partnership and in harmony with the will of God. Planning for the future, when it is carefully mixed with much prayer, can generate excitement, commitment and far deeper faith. When a group of Christians work together on God's agenda and always put him first, the Holy Spirit can really work powerfully.

Priorities

Yet again, Jesus is asking us about our priorities. When the chips were down the manager realized that people mattered more than money. Their friendship could last a lifetime but money would soon melt away. The manager looked ahead, just as we always need to, and saw what really mattered.

So this parable challenges our zealousness. Many of us work longer and longer hours. We see less and less of our families and friends and in any spare time we plan how we can get even more possessions. Yet we are only here on earth for such a short time. So why do we not look forward? Do we live as if we have understood our priorities and planned how we will respond to them? Or does a downpour or an important match on the television stop us going to worship God? How determined are we, how enthusiastic? Compare the joy of seeing your team score in a football match with the joy of knowing that you are saved, free, spotless and perfect and are going to heaven when you die. Now compare the reactions at a football stadium and in most churches!

We are also called to face up to reality. The manager saw his situation, faced up to it and did something positive about it. He did not just write himself off and lie around feeling sorry for himself. Neither did he sit there waiting for some 'miraculous' solution, as if God would simply take him out of the mess his own actions had got him into. He took a good look at himself and acknowledged his failings but also recognized the gifts God had given him. He then set about using them.

The parable shows that we should use the material possessions God has given us so generously, in order to develop friendships. When reverses occur, and they inevitably will, these are the friends who will rally round us. Money is not evil. Trying to live without it usually means people will have to rely on charity to survive. Most of us, if we are honest, are much more likely to become servants of money, wanting more of it for ourselves.

Using money for good

As good Christian stewards, however, we need to see money as what it really is: a very useful resource and something we can use to benefit others as well as ourselves. By using money and things in the right way we will neither hate them nor worship them but use them to bring love and hope into the lives of other people. We have to think of their future as we think of our own – in terms of immediate need, but even more importantly in terms of their eternal calling.

It is important that we look for clouds on the horizon and prepare for them, otherwise we will be like those caught in debt who do nothing until they are taken to court or their goods are repossessed. If we listen to the weather forecast and know it is going to rain later we can take a raincoat or an umbrella with us, or postpone the picnic till tomorrow. With no planning, things are easily ruined, and if we are in charge, people will be much less inclined to believe us or go with us again in the future.

Actions are all important

Just as the manager in the story shows, the best way of demonstrating a change of heart is by altering the way we act. In millions of people's lives in our society today, money is not just a rival to God; it has become the most important thing there is. It is a god that many both worship and covet. It encourages selfishness and is potentially so damaging. This is why Jesus asks us to show through our actions that we hold on to money and things lightly as we worship him deeply. And more than this, he warns us not to worship a rival that could prevent us entering the Kingdom of heaven.

'You cannot serve both God and money' seems to be a saying that Jesus was very fond of! Serving money makes us selfish, and we can't serve God and be selfish at the same time. So the way we handle money is a very clear indication of our real commitment to Christ.

Real treasure

The concluding words of this story are truly sobering for all of us. As Christians we are called to a total experience. We cannot select the verses we have highlighted in our Bible and just ignore the other verses we are not very keen on! We acknowledge God's love as we determinedly seek his will, knowing that he can provide the resources.

We gladly use those resources by taking personal risks for the benefit of others with real needs, but we do so with proper planning and forward thinking.

It is important that we see how Jesus sees things on earth as 'small' but in heaven as 'great'. Equally we need to hold on to the truth that what we do on earth will affect our place in heaven. By not putting people before possessions on earth we may find we have very little 'treasure' in heaven. By being obedient in the small everyday things and having our priorities in line with God's we will be storing up wonderful eternal treasures.

So it is impossible to serve two masters. As we follow Jesus, we need to be open to change, and this will help us grow. Our journey never ends at a particular time. Each day we need to seek to be just that little bit closer to Jesus than we were the day before.

The Pharisees in Jesus' day would not welcome such teaching. They liked their position of power and all the wealth that went with it. It made them feel superior, and despite the teaching that exposed their shallowness they were not prepared to change their ways. As Christians we have to ensure that we do not fall into the same trap. If we really want to know Jesus and totally commit to him, rather than flirt with money, we will soon be engulfed in an all-embracing passion that will make us truly and eternally rich beyond description!

17. Musical Chairs

Luke 7:31–35

> To what can I compare the people of today? What are we like? We are just like children sitting at a party and calling out to each other, 'We played musical chairs but you refused to join in. You said you wanted to play "pass the parcel" but again you didn't do so when we played.'
>
> We are always so quick to justify our position. For when John the Baptist came, who didn't eat bread or drink wine, people said of him, 'There's something the matter with him. He must have a demon.' Yet when Jesus came along eating and drinking, they said, 'Here is a glutton and a drunkard, a friend of tax collectors and "sinners".' We need to demonstrate what wisdom we have been given.

Behaving like spoilt children

Have you ever tried to organize a children's party? If you have not planned all the games, as soon as they arrive, one wants to do one thing and another something else. A couple will be sulking and not wanting to play anything. Some will not like your food and others will spill their drink in the excitement of it all. Unless firm control is taken and you carry the children with you, things can rapidly degenerate into chaos.

This parable demonstrates the importance of having meaning and hope in one's life. Children who constantly squabble for no good reason have no direction. We are exactly the same. We want our way: we believe it is best. We simply do not hear the points of view of others.

Even in the church, sadly, we have disputes. 'Let's get rid of the pews.' 'No. They've been here for years.' 'I can't hear the organ.' 'The organ is too loud.' 'Let's get rid of the organ and have a worship group.'

'Everyone, without exception, should tithe.' 'No one should tithe. We are under grace, not law.'

'We should let anyone who wants to use our building.' 'We should open up our building to other Christian groups.' 'This is our church. Why should we have to clear up someone else's mess?'

Beginning to get the picture? Where is God in all this? As we seek his way, surely we need to come together and seek his face. If everything is God's and belongs to him, not us, it must follow that we need to follow his plans and not our own.

We will not win an argument by shouting words like 'God told me' at each other. Rather we need to be on our knees next to each other, listening and waiting for God to truly let us know his will.

Carrying out God's purpose

Jesus wanted to show that often the people of God do not carry out the purpose of God. Rather than trying to develop his priorities, it is easier for us to stick in our own little huddles with our own narrow prejudices. The church service is too 'high' or too 'low'. The sermon is too long, too short or too irrelevant. Just like little children we want to play with our toys when we like, we want to have our own 'considered' views, and we do not want anyone else to tell us what to do. Not even God.

This is why we are so reluctant to be really good stewards of the many blessings that God pours out on us. It is much easier to pretend that things are 'mine' so that I can do what I like with them. But God is both Creator and Owner of everything on earth. Once we accept this it becomes so much easier to be good stewards of these resources, readily submitting to him because he has a keen interest in every part of life.

Emptying ourselves

This is why, unlike the children in the parable, who are just full of themselves, we have to empty ourselves of all selfish desires and thoughts. It is only when we are empty that God is able to fill us with good things. Imagine a bowl full to the brim with bad fruit. It is no good trying to put fresh new fruit on top of the bad fruit; it will simply fall off. Even when there is some good fruit mixed with the bad it is unlikely to be seen clearly, because the bad fruit will put people off. Only a bowl full of fresh fruit will truly appeal. Similarly, it is only when we empty ourselves of all 'our' desires that God is able to fill us with his Holy Spirit and make us truly attractive.

In Philippians 2:5–11 we read that Jesus emptied himself and became as a servant. It is impossible for us to become servants of Christ if we still see ourselves as masters of our own destiny. By emptying ourselves we are acknowledging Jesus as Saviour and Lord.

One of the main reasons why we criticize others and look down on them is that we do not have a clear sense of purpose. Our purpose is to show Jesus' love, grace and forgiveness to hurting individuals. We can do this in the sure confidence that we are going to heaven when we die and that Jesus is already leading us along the right path.

Have confidence in Christ

It is this confidence in Jesus, not in ourselves, that should give us comfort and assurance and enable us to be loving and caring towards others. If we are always putting God first and our neighbours before ourselves, we will definitely be on the right lines.

I am sure that many of my most cherished beliefs will be exploded the second I arrive in heaven. Some of the things I argued about so strongly will seem unimportant. I am also sure that I will be surprised by some who are in heaven. But I know that the person least deserving to be there will be myself.

So can you rise above the arguments of everyday events? Do you have a vision that is in line with God's – even if you are unsure whether this is what you would choose if left to your own devices? Do we pray quietly for God's will to be done and wait for him to reply? Are we prepared to surrender our own wants so that God's purpose can be carried out, not just in our own lives but also in the much wider world?

Jesus tells us not to stand up for our rights, but rather to seek out our responsibilities as a true follower of Christ. We are not to be like little children wanting their own way: we should always seek his way. He promises that we will never regret it!

18. Night Shift

Matthew 25:1–13

The kingdom of heaven will be like ten taxi drivers who were out working for a firm on the night shift. Five of them were sensible and ensured that their tanks were always full of petrol, but the five others reasoned that it was unlikely a long journey would be called for without warning at night, so they never bothered to fill their tanks for such a shift. At three in the morning there was jesting among them and some moaning about it being such a quiet night. Others simply dozed in the taxi office.

Suddenly there was a burst of activity on the phones. An international flight had been diverted to the local airport and people wanted to be transported all over the country. These were fares available that the drivers rarely even dreamt of. They all rushed to their cabs, but the five with nearly empty tanks said to the others, 'Give us some of your petrol. We barely have enough even to get us to the airport.'

'No,' they replied. 'We'll have to go a long way in the middle of the night and we'll need full tanks to get us to our destinations. You will have to go and see if you can find a petrol station open somewhere, but we don't know of any that open for several hours.'

While they were waiting for the petrol station to open, the others arrived at the airport and were able to pick up all the passengers who needed transport.

Later, the other five taxis arrived but could not find anyone looking for them. 'We're here now,' they called out in desperation. 'We can go with you now.'

A carpenter was working nearby. 'Everybody who wanted to travel has already taken one of the taxis that came earlier. I'm afraid you've missed your chance.'

Therefore watch out, because you do not have even the slightest idea of when the time will come and you need to be prepared and ready.

This is a simple parable and needs little by way of explanation. We need to be ready for Christ's return. We cannot say with any certainty, as some do, that Christ will come back in our lifetime. This has been said for two thousand years and the early disciples who knew Jesus on earth expected his return before they died. Nevertheless we are to live as if his return is imminent.

This state of readiness has numerous implications in terms of what our priorities should be on earth. It should be a factor in our relationships, as well as in our handling of time, money and all the other talents God has given us.

We have been chosen by God and at some time have made a commitment to him, but our spiritual condition is entirely down to us. Does Christ come first in our lives, do we put others' needs before our wants, and do we ask concerning all major issues, 'What would Jesus do?'

Are we living in such a way that we would be fully prepared should Jesus appear before us this moment? This could either be here on earth as Jesus returns, or in heaven if we suddenly died. Have we said all the words of love, thanks and forgiveness that we want to? Have we put right any strained or broken relationships? Have we returned the things we should have returned a long time ago? Are we at peace and ready to meet our Maker?

The petrol in this story represents the Holy Spirit, who should be always overflowing within us. Without him we rapidly become dry and literally 'run out of fuel'. We need to keep on being open to God and always be ready for when he calls us.

Once Jesus returns, or when we die, we will be unable to put right things that are still outstanding on earth. As we go about our daily lives we need to carry this at the forefront of our minds. We should do so not out of fear but out of the real hope of meeting Jesus and the desire to be at peace and friends with everyone we know.

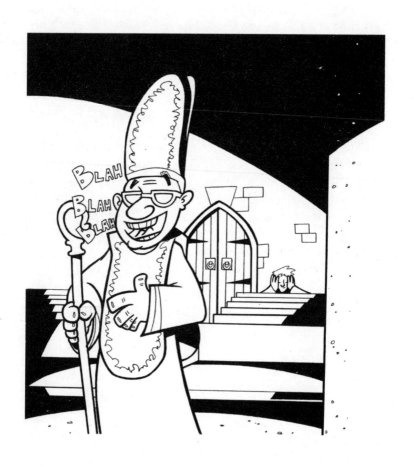

19. Bishop's Move

Luke 18:9–14

For those who are confident in their own 'goodness' and look down on everybody else, here is a story to jolt us back to reality.

A bishop stood at the altar rail. He was wearing his full regalia and looked very comfortable there. In a loud voice and holding his head high, he began to pray: 'God, I thank you that you have given me special revelation and special blessing. I am not like other men – adulterers, thieves and sinners – nor even like this bookmaker. I fast once a week, ensure that I tithe every penny of my income, and am always telling you in prayer how good I am.'

The bookmaker was sitting in the back pew. Tears were streaming down his face. Kneeling before God and not daring to look up to heaven, he pleaded, 'God, have mercy on me. I have done so much wrong and need you so much.'

I need to tell you that this man, rather than the other, went home justified before God. For everyone who thinks he is superior will be brought down, while those who truly acknowledge their shortcomings and repent of them before God will be exalted.

Dangers of superficial faith

Putting on a 'show' comes so easily to us. We want to impress others all the time. It may be we want to boast, indirectly of course, about our wealth or our power. So we drive around in expensive cars, wear the latest fashions and have every piece of electrical equipment that has ever been invented. Alternatively we may just drop into the conversation how much better our holiday destination was than the one visited by the person who was just speaking, or we might just mention a few household names in the conversation to let people know how well connected we are.

As Christians we can be just the same. It is so easy to go and hear a well-known speaker as if somehow his spirituality will wash off on us. But we ignore the less famous speaker in the small local church who has been faithfully serving God for years. In doing so, we actually force the speakers to become more like entertainers than teachers of God's truth. Sadly the end result of this in many cases is that our faith demands what we demand from our television sets – shallow amusement which we 'enjoy' but forget five minutes later.

Dangers of self-justification

We can look down on the single mum and criticize her for 'wasting' her money on lottery tickets in a desperate attempt to improve the lot of her children, but justify our spending on private health and education in the same breath.

Some Christian leaders are sadly not immune from this either. Constantly mixing with their own kind, they create a 'holy huddle' where there is a tendency to continually promote each other, each inviting the other to their own conferences (no expense spared, of course), with the bills picked up by naive and gullible congregations. This constant navel-gazing and seeking of approval from people who think the same as you and may even rely on your support is very dangerous.

The sad truth is that if these two men were at a Christian conference, the bishop would be on the platform and the bookmaker would be kept hidden away. Let me say straightaway that I have made this character a bishop only to illustrate the point. It could be any Christian convinced that their commitment and good works make them somehow superior to others. Unfortunately there is a bit of this in all of us.

In this particular story the bishop didn't really go to church to talk to God. It was part of his ritual, and he wanted everyone else in the church to know he was a really good guy. He did not humbly fall on his knees before God and seek forgiveness. Rather he talked *at* God as if to remind him of all his good works and to ensure himself an exalted place in heaven.

We are sinners!

The bookmaker just knew that he was screwed up. He saw the despair of gamblers spending money needed desperately for the family food bill on horses that were a 'certainty' but usually weren't. He saw the hopelessness in their eyes and yet by doing his job he was allowing their problems to continue. In the original telling of the parable, Jesus spoke of a tax collector who would charge way over the minimum required (just as Zacchaeus did) and would feather his own nest with the misfortune of others.

Self-righteousness is so dangerous. It easily leads to pride and a feeling of superiority. This belief that we have got it together makes it extremely hard for us to hear from God, even when he is shouting at us that we haven't! Every one of us needs to pray like the bookmaker and we need to do so every day. I am truly ashamed of the sins I committed before becoming a Christian, but quite honestly, even the sins that I am aware of having committed since then make me want to curl up in a corner and die.

I need God's mercy, protection and forgiveness every moment of the day. And so do we all. Please never let pride in your achievements get in the way of a close and loving relationship with God. After all, it is he who has given you these gifts and talents in the first place.

The story demonstrates that it is possible to be committed in the wrong way. We can try to show 'commitment' by keeping all the rules. If we achieve this we naturally tend to feel superior to those who 'do not bother' to do so. Yet we can go to all the right meetings, lead in prayer, give regularly and still miss the point. Our acts of commitment have to be supported by our basic understanding of just how much God loves us. It is this sacrificial love of Jesus for me, for you and for others that is central to our faith. What we do does not alter by one jot the amount of love he has for us.

Things done out of duty will cause resentment and will eventually fail. Actions that bubble out of the joy of knowing the freedom of real forgiveness will last. Things we do out of self-belief make us arrogant; things done out of genuine love for God release us.

Our society today thinks like the first of these two men. What we have and what we wear on the surface seems more important than who we really are and what we do away from the limelight. If we try to keep the rules in order to show that we are good, we may fool ourselves and others but we will not fool God. We may concentrate so hard on not doing 'bad' things that we lose all sense of compassion for others whom we see 'failing' around us. It may then come as a bit of a shock to us when we get to heaven and we are not asked, 'What did you *not* do?' but rather, 'What did *you do* to help others?' Something to reflect on.

20. Too Busy

Matthew 21:28–32

There was a man who had two sons. He went to the first and said, 'Son, I am decorating the outside of the house today. Will you come and help me?'

'Sorry,' he answered, 'I am too busy watching the sport.' But he reflected on this for a few minutes and then changed his mind and went to help his father.

The father went to the other son and said the same thing. He answered, 'Of course I will help you.' But he got distracted and did not go.

Which of the two did as the father wanted?

Actions, not words

This parable illustrates something we all know: what we do is much more important than what we say. Paying lip service to our faith gets us nowhere fast: in fact it is worse than saying nothing. Our words appear empty, and if we are not living out our faith in a sure and certain hope we are actively undermining any witness to Christ that others may be receiving.

Today, just as in Jesus' day, there are people saying they want to be obedient to God's calling. Some may even be boasting or trying to demonstrate how well they do this and how close to God they have become. So people suddenly develop a 'holy' voice as they speak to God, or spend ages over grace at the dinner table when they would not normally say a word if important guests weren't there. Well, that's got me condemned!

Seriously though, our faith is just too important for us merely to go through the motions. There is absolutely no point in doing so. God knows our true feelings and intentions and he calls us to a living faith, to be salt and light in a world of darkness, and with our actions always to point towards his goodness and grace.

21. Counting the Cost

Luke 14:25–35

There is a huge and personal cost in following Jesus. Sometimes you may have to put him above your father and mother, your spouse and your children. Never deny him, even if it means losing your life. This is the cost of being his disciple. Whoever does not carry the cross and follow Jesus cannot really be his disciple.

If you're planning to spend money on a conservatory, surely you will first sit down and estimate the cost, to see whether you have enough to complete it. Otherwise you'll end up with the builders laying the foundation but then simply walking away because you can't pay them any more. People who see it will ridicule you, saying, 'This fool began to build but hadn't planned his finances properly and wasn't able to finish.'

What country that has a dispute with another country does not first consider the strength of its armed forces before going to war? If they realize that the other country is much more powerful than they are, the weaker country will do everything it can to settle things diplomatically. In the same way, none of you can become the disciple of

Jesus if you do not give up the ownership of all 'your' possessions.

Salt is no use if it's not fresh. Nor is it any good if it's left in its little pot. It needs to be mixed with food to give it taste and make it more pleasurable.

Let those who really want to follow Jesus hear this, understand it and then put it into action.

Trusting

The simplest way of responding to this story is to take a look at the way we handle money in this country. Or even more challengingly, to look at the way Christians handle money in this country. At a deeper level the story is about how we trust in our own resources rather than handing everything over to God and trusting him. This is so strange. Christians acknowledge that Jesus is Lord and are happy to sing 'I surrender all', but then refuse to surrender anything that has to do with money. There is a cost to following Jesus but also a huge eternal reward. We are called to share his cross in this life so that we can share his crown in the next. Are we living in this reality today?

The cost of following Jesus

This parable shows the cost of discipleship in a way that cannot be misunderstood. We are called to give Jesus first place in every part of our lives. So our relationships with our families, work, time and money are all subjugated to our relationship with Christ. At the end of the day this is about total commitment.

On the one hand we need to be aware of the cost of following Jesus, as it certainly can cause tensions on earth if we are doing this in any real sense, and on the other we need to realize that it is only by turning to God for help that we can find the resources we need to get us through. So if, as we pray, we hear God call us to do something, we can be sure he will provide the resources. If we try to do something in our own strength without asking him first we can easily fail.

Being good stewards

This is why we are called to be good stewards of all that God has given us to manage. If we do this we do not have to worry about lacking, as God's resources never run dry. This is why the way we handle money is an acid test of our commitment to him and of how effective we really are as disciples.

Here are some things to do when we think we need to buy something new:

1 Turn to God, not your credit card.
2 Ask him if you really need it.
3 Give him time to reply.
4 Look at your budget to see whether you can afford it now.
5 Be prepared to wait if not – but if you are clear that God has said you do need it, ask him to provide the resources.
6 Make sure you are talking and praying about this together with your partner.

Making a difference in our world

Are you a salty Christian? By this I mean are you being Jesus to your community and taking your message of hope and joy out to a world that increasingly knows Jesus only as a swear word? Salt is incredibly useful but it is not much good when it's just sitting in the pot with other grains of salt. Yes, sometimes several grains of salt are more helpful than just one – but only if they come out of the pot!

We are called to give meaning to the lives of many who are wandering through this world like sheep without a shepherd. It is important to remember that though we are in a minority in this country, a little salt goes an awfully long way.

A living church

What is true for us as individual Christians is also true for the church as a whole. The church is meant to be a vibrant and living sign of the Gospel, not a desperate appeal for more funds through a giant thermometer poster by the door. The church is not called upon to develop endless building projects unless there has been a clear mandate to many from God. Look again as this parable is retold:

> Suppose a church wanted to build an extension. Would they first not sit down and calculate how this would be used for the entire community which they serve? Would they not ensure that there was no other building nearby, especially another church building, that they could share

to reduce costs? If not, would they not then get accurate estimates of what was affordable and at all times ensure there were enough pledges and cash to complete it? Because if they laid the foundation and then ran out of money or had to borrow expensively from the bank, people would say, 'How foolish they look. They just expected that their God would wave a wand and all would be well.'

Looking out

How many times have you heard over the years those familiar words, 'God will provide'? Sadly, what this often means is that people glibly spend on the whims of today, without any reference to God's wishes, and neglect the needs of tomorrow or even of the world around them. If building an extension is part of God's plan, he will show it to all the key leaders of the church. One thing he will not do is encourage significant spending to make the 'club' more comfortable for its members! Our churches are meant to be beacons of light in an otherwise increasingly dark world. We are meant to be looking outwards and upwards, not inwards. So what does our church notice board say? Does Matins 10.30 a.m. or Eucharist at 6 o'clock mean anything to anyone who is passing by? But 'We have family, bereavement and debt counsellors' might. The addresses and/or phone numbers of the nearest Citizen's Advice, Relate and Samaritans would also be useful. If we expect the 'food' to come to the 'salt' we will have a long wait. Let's get out there and show them just how much tastier their lives could become!

Thinking outside our box

We have to be demonstrating good stewardship to our community and our world. How can we really spend millions of pounds on building projects that are essentially inward looking when every two seconds a child dies of starvation, and still call ourselves Christian? Nearly all Christians in the west spell sin 'sex'. Of course sexual sin is wrong, but then so is financial sin, selfishness and judgementalism. Money is a precious commodity. Just like water, there needs to be enough of it to go round. Focus too much on ourselves and ignore the needs of others and we will be soon in the same place as the Pharisees.

Remember the figures I gave earlier, that the three hundred richest people in the world have more accumulated wealth than the poorest 50 per cent of the world's population. Or, even worse, that the three richest people have more than the forty-eight poorest countries! This is obscene. Yet such a gap between rich and poor is not only found in this world; it is found in this country. It is not only in our communities; it is in our churches. Many people live on benefits and low incomes. Frankly, I do not know how they manage week in, week out. But millions more of us buy things we don't need with money we don't have to impress people we don't even like! Over the Christmas period we in this country borrowed an extra £11 billion to buy presents and extra food. This sum of money would have fed and clothed fifty million people in the Third World for a year. I think we should perhaps consider repenting over this, don't you?

So, as Christians, we need to take this parable very much to heart. We need to make God central in every part of our lives and be really sure that when we are spending we are doing so with his full support and all his resources behind us. Failure to do so will leave us in a mess, looking foolish and having no value whatsoever as salt in this tasteless and shallow world.

We all live for today and fail to show true unconditional love to those less fortunate than ourselves. And I know this starts with me. Please, Lord, help me to be a good steward. Help me, Lord, to be more like Jesus every day – because he gave everything for me.

22. Owing Me, Owing You

Matthew 18:21–35

Forgiveness is never easy, but it is always essential. Furthermore it is something we have to keep on doing, because we keep on hurting Jesus far more than we are ever hurt. Despite our best efforts, we keep on sinning, and in effect every time we do this we are hammering another nail into Jesus on the cross. Compared with this, anything that anyone has done to upset me is inconsequential.

Nor is this about 'How many times?' When Peter heard Jesus tell the original parable, he thought this was what it was all about. He expressed a lot more forgiveness, but Jesus demands total forgiveness – and he does so solely for our benefit.

Here is a story to underline the importance of forgiveness.

The kingdom of heaven is like this. A charity trustee was talking to one of his directors. He gently brought up the subject of what was happening in the charity and wanted to know why the director seemed to be under such stress. At first, the director tried to bluff his way through, but then he came clean: 'I am in such a mess. I have purchased too expensive a house and filled it with too many things, and my family is really struggling. I think the house will be repossessed soon and then we will be left with nothing,' he said. 'But I'm sure I'll be able to pay it back eventually,' he stammered. 'It's just a question of waiting and hoping for something to happen.'

The charity trustee asked how much was owed and ascertained that a figure of £20,000 would clear all the debts. He had just had a legacy of about that amount and felt sorry for the man, and especially his family.

'I need to talk to my wife about this and pray things through,' he said, 'but I have just come into some money and I am mindful to help you settle your debts. Come and see me after the church service on Sunday.'

The charity director was elated but before the staff meeting that day he took aside a young assistant and, grasping her by the neck, pinned her against the wall in the kitchen, saying, 'You promised me that £50 back that I lent you last month. I'm having a really lucky week, so it must be my turn to win the lottery. Give me the money you owe me now, or I will have to take you to court and I will personally see that you are thrown out of this charity. There's no place for thieves in the family of God.'

The person in question was a single mum who was barely able to survive. In fact she did so by cleaning the trustee's house once a week. The following day she was doing her job but it was clear to the trustee that something was troubling her.

'What's the matter?' he asked her gently. 'It looks like you haven't slept a wink and you've been crying a lot.'

With many tears the whole sorry story soon emerged. The trustee was appalled. Firstly he gave a gift to the young lady to help her through her current financial plight. Then he summoned the charity director to him.

'I just cannot believe that you would be so evil as to pursue the small amount of money owed to you by someone who is quite clearly struggling even to survive. But to do it just after I'd told you I was thinking of clearing *all* your huge debts is astonishing. Given what has happened I have no intention of giving you a penny, and what is more you have quite clearly demonstrated that you are unfit to be in any leadership role in this organisation.'

You all really need to take this in and learn to forgive your fellow human beings completely and from your heart. If not, it will be impossible for our Father to forgive us.

Forgive others

The conclusion to this parable is central to our belief and the conclusion Jesus draws from it cannot be repeated often enough. Yet it really is hard to live it out! Can I really grasp that Jesus' forgiveness of me is directly linked to the way I react to other people – especially those who have upset or offended me? Yet I easily pray these words in the Lord's Prayer: 'Father, forgive us our sins as [in the same fashion as] we forgive those who sin against us.' Because it is so difficult, Jesus keeps repeating the message throughout his teaching. He means it to hit home hard. Have we truly grasped it?

You see, anything that anyone has done to me in my lifetime, be it gossiping, lying, going behind my back or whatever, is inconsequential compared with what my sin has done to Jesus. I might have received wounded pride because of others. Jesus has received fatal wounds because of my self-centredness.

In the original version, this story starts with Peter trying to show Jesus that he has a forgiving heart, that he is prepared to forgive someone seven times whereas the Jewish law limited this to three. Peter was effectively boasting to Jesus, 'Look at me! Look at how godly I am.' He was trying to impress Jesus with his words and with his sums. But forgiveness is not about words and arithmetic, it is about love and compassion in action. So the message of this parable is always to have a forgiving heart.

Never forget your forgiveness

The parable uses extremes to highlight the points being made. The charity director owed a large debt, in fact so large that it would be impossible to pay back without years and years of real sacrifice. The strains that this would have put on the family are immense, and many relationships today are breaking down under such strain. But the man did not see it like that. He just 'hoped' things would somehow miraculously get better. With the interest accumulating at a rapid rate, however, this would be highly unlikely. He was living in cloud cuckoo land and did nothing to try to rectify the situation by budgeting or reigning in his spending. The fact that he later thought of spending £50 on the lottery clearly shows just how misplaced his thinking was!

Despite the size of the debt, the trustee demonstrated real compassion. He could have told the man not to worry about his giving to the church, or even that he was prepared to offer a loan. Instead he mentioned that he was going to consider clearing the entire debt. There was no obligation to do this whatsoever. This was a free gift. This is why it was right of him not to react to the emotion of the moment and give the money there and then. He needed to talk to his wife about it and then in prayer with her ask God for his guidance in this matter. It is always right to ask God before rushing off and using money, whether spending or even on occasions giving. After all, God wants obedient followers, not emotional ones – and at the end of the day it is his money in the first place!

This is how God our Father reaches us. He offers us something we dare not ask for, as it is simply too huge a picture to grasp. It is also something we could never earn. Our shortcomings and failings are simply washed away by unconditional love. There is no resentment, no claim for restitution, nor is it grudgingly given. But this forgiveness is not easy. It carries enormous cost.

Once pardoned, we do not have to worry that God will remind us of our failings. He will never remind us of those things that could never deserve to be forgiven. The only way we can close the door on receiving true forgiveness is when we fail to show it to others. The whole concept of forgiveness suggests that we have some to give as well as some to receive. By holding grudges and nursing our own resentments, all we do is cause much self-inflicted damage.

Remember others' needs

In the parable the charity director who has just been released from a near impossible debt reacts without mercy to someone who owes him a trifling amount. What is even worse is the fact that the single mum in question needs the money to feed the children: he needs it only to gamble. He even says, 'Give me the money you owe to me now,' as if it is generally understood that everyone should always repay their debts on demand. Given that he thinks all his debts are about to be cleared by someone else, this is grimly ironic, to put it mildly!

The single mum is in a similar situation to that of the charity director, but there are important differences. She owes far less and she earns far less, and is struggling to meet the needs of her family. The biggest difference, however, is in the way she is treated.

No wonder the trustee reacted angrily when he heard what had happened. How relieved he must have felt that he hadn't acted immediately and given the money when it was first mentioned. He had tried to demonstrate the forgiveness of God and had it slapped back in his face.

Mercy received must be reflected in mercy shown. As I mentioned earlier, any wrongs we have suffered are inconsequential compared with the things we already have had forgiven. William Shakespeare put it like this:

And earthly power doth then show likest God's
When mercy seasons justice. Therefore, Jew,
Though justice be thy plea, consider this:
That in the course of justice none of us
Should see salvation. We do pray for mercy,
And that same prayer doth teach us all to render
The deeds of mercy.

(The Merchant of Venice, Act 4, Scene 1)

Never judge

In this parable the charity director interpreted the offer of having his debts cleared as something personal. It was for him alone. He must have thought he was some sort of favourite of the trustee. Perhaps it was this very thinking, that he was somebody special, that persuaded him to demand that the woman's trivial debt be paid back. This thinking and his lack of charity only go to show both his selfishness and his stupidity.

But to a greater or lesser degree we can all behave like this man. We so often demand standards from others that we are incapable of reaching ourselves. We spend all our time criticizing others while at the same time we justify ourselves. So we condemn the homosexual while we lust after the wife next door. We who are happily married can look down on those going through divorce, yet we continue to spend and spend on trivia as children die of hunger. We get outraged at the thought of a young girl living on benefits deciding after much turmoil to have an abortion – so much so that we write a letter to complain about it from our house which has just been valued at over one million pounds.

I can see your splinter but not my plank. What is pigheaded stubbornness in you is righteous steadfastness in me. Your bluntness is my frankness. Your meanness my thrift. And if I ever do fall short of those perfect standards, I can give you at least ten good reasons why other people and outside influences have caused this to happen! If only we 'loved our neighbours as ourselves' and were as considerate to them as we are to ourselves, we would have far fewer disputes and we all would be a lot happier.

The world says 'revenge is sweet', but the pleasure won't last and soon it will leave a bitter taste in the mouth. Unforgiveness soon leads to mental, emotional and even physical and spiritual pain. Our imagined hurts get magnified to such an extent that God's healing words cannot be heard. Revenge is not sweet: it is immensely damaging, which is why Jesus spoke so much against it and even died so we could grasp the full meaning of forgiveness. Our forgiveness has to be total. We have to forgive and forget (however hard this may appear) – otherwise we have not forgiven. We need to move on, however hard this is. R.T. Kendall says, 'Keep no record of wrongs and *never* try to vindicate yourself.' This is such sound advice.

In fact, when we do not forgive, and therefore disobey God, we are not so much breaking his rules as breaking his heart. If we break the law there are penalties we can pay to atone for our wrongdoing. But we cannot mend a broken heart. The only way ahead is to show that we fully grasp what the love of God has done for each of us, particularly as demonstrated through the death of Jesus at Calvary, and then we need to freely forgive those who have hurt us in any way.

Are there people you are still holding grudges against? People who have hurt you in thought, word or deed? Are you even, as in this parable, still bearing a grudge over money or things lent to someone who promised to return them but hasn't? If so, joyfully accept that their need must be far greater than yours. And even if that is not the case, the matter is between them and God, not them and you.

Don't go over the top and proffer your forgiveness to someone who has no idea that they have upset you in any way! But where you know there are tensions, where others feel guilty, try to stretch out your hand of forgiveness today. If this is you, please put the book down and make the call or write the letter now. I will never forget the look of a lady who rushed up to see me because she had just phoned her dad for the first time in twelve years. The tears of freedom on her face told the whole story. This could be you in a matter of minutes!

23. Tenant Trouble

Matthew 21:33–45, Mark 12:1–12, Luke 20:9–19

There was a landowner who built a house on some land he owned. He built it to the highest specifications and no expense was spared. All the latest equipment was fitted in the kitchen, and he added a conservatory and a landscaped garden. Then he rented out his dream home, as he had to work abroad for several years. However, when the rent became due it was not paid and so he sent an agent to get it.

The tenants were enjoying the house and treating it as if it was theirs. They saw no reason to pay for it, so when the agent arrived he was sent away with a flea in his ear. Another agent came and was threatened with violence, and a third was actually hit as he tried to reason with them. Eventually, in desperation, the landlord called his son and asked him to visit. 'I know they will respect him,' he thought.

But when the tenants saw the son they said to each other, 'This is the heir. He is the landlord's only son. If we kill him and hide his body, his father will be more concerned about trying to find his son than he will be about bothering to collect rent. We will be able to live here for free and do as we please.' So the tenants grabbed hold of the son, took him in their car a long way from the house, then killed him and hid his body.

Now, do you really expect the owner to do nothing? What do you think the landlord should do? We are probably all in agreement on this.

The landlord knew how the tenants had behaved towards the agents and that his son had been last seen heading to his house to confront them. He should tell the police, so that the tenants will be arrested and lose their freedom for ever. Good riddance to them. The landlord will then rent out the house to good tenants who will look after his property and pay him what is due to him at all times.

But Jesus gently reminds us, 'Have you forgotten the Scriptures? The person that the people rejected became the key player.'

The Kingdom of God will be given to people who acknowledge God by their actions in all that they do. The person who acknowledges God may have to be broken, as Jesus becomes the building block for the rest of their life, but the one who shows by his actions that he has chosen to ignore God's teaching will eventually be crushed.

When religious people hear these parables they secretly realize that he is talking about them.

Different tenants

People who have rented out their homes tell me that there is a wide divergence in the way tenants behave. Some keep the home in pristine condition, pay for any damage that they do, always pay the rent on time and leave the house in a better state than when they moved in to it. Some will pay the rent but always be on the lookout for things that are wrong or will want various items replacing. Others simply have no respect for the property or the items within it. They seem to think they have a right to be there, and even when they don't pay the rent they still believe they can do what they want with the property and even trash it should they feel like it.

Before we rush off and criticize this last group we need to stop and think for a moment. How do we treat God's property? Do we take the many good things we have for granted? Even worse, do we take the death of Jesus on the cross for granted, barely thinking about his suffering as we go about our daily lives?

The people in the parable

In this parable the landlord is God and the house represents the people of God. The tenants are those who have been chosen to look after God's world and the agents represent the prophets sent by God to point out how they should be behaving but who are ignored or rejected. The son is of course Jesus himself.

So the parable shows God's ongoing patience with his people, their continuing rejection of him, his prophets and his Word. The story culminates in the sending of the only son, his betrayal and murder. Finally God ensures justice is done, with those who rejected his son facing ridicule and suffering.

The perfect landlord

Think for a moment about the land before the house was built. It would probably be barren and uneven. There would be rocks and many weeds. The land would have to be smoothed and all impediments swept away. Then it would need to be fenced for protection. Deep and sound foundations would need to be laid so that there was no subsidence. The property would need to be built with real care to ensure the wind and rain did not adversely affect the occupants. Then the property would be fitted out with all the essential gadgets to ensure that everyone in the house could cook, eat, bathe and sleep. The landlord loved that house. He loved every part of it. To him it was not a house; it was a sign of his love and commitment. It was a home. Everything that could have been done had been done, and so it should have been a sign of love to anyone who ever came remotely near it.

At the deeper level, everything has been done for us and freely given to us. What is more, we have many more things than the vast majority of people throughout history have even dreamt of. How responsibly are we taking these privileges? Do we really acknowledge that all we have is from God, and do we genuinely and continually thank him for all the preparations he has made and the things he has done for us in this wonderful life?

The choices we face

The story also highlights the fact that each one of us has choices to make. We can do good or evil; we can follow him or follow our own selfish motives. The landlord left the property in perfect condition and with everything that was needed to enable the tenants' lives to run smoothly. But the landlord left the tenants to it. He did not live next door and come round every five minutes to see what they were doing. They were totally free. All that was expected of them was to pay the rent when it was due and keep the property in good condition. They could use the garden, grow vegetables or flowers, and also cook whatever they liked when they liked.

Acknowledging God for who he is

But the tenants became greedy. They had no respect for the landlord who had provided all this for them in the first place. Soon they were regarding the property as their own. They didn't need permission to knock down a few walls or live in a tip if that is what they chose to do. Why should they pay rent? After all, they were making 'improvements' to the property. Their initial rebellion began to escalate as agents appeared, reminding them of what their responsibilities were. This eventually culminated in the killing of the landlord's only son. By then their reasoning had become completely twisted. They believed they could literally get away with murder in order to carry on living selfishly.

It is so easy for sin to grow quickly once it has taken root. The tenants were probably not idle. They went to work and earned money. They just wanted to have it all to themselves. They might well have argued that as the value of the property increased, this was due to the 'improvements' they had made to it, so why should the landlord take the profit?

God is trusting us

In this parable the landlord trusted the tenants. He would have had a legal contract agreed and signed by both parties, so he would anticipate that they would stick to their side of the bargain as he stuck to his. He employed an agent to make it easier for the tenants to pay rather than having to transfer money to him directly overseas. But as the rent never started to arrive, he had to send the agents to find out why. At first they were probably fobbed off with excuses: 'Oh, I thought John had done it,' or 'The cheque is in the post'. Once they got away with that, the boldness of the tenants increased, and so each time an agent appeared they got just that little bit more aggressive and intimidating. By now they may have been thinking about how they might bully the landlord or so frighten him that he would stop pursuing them for the rent. Eventually they would gain squatters' rights over the property and it would become theirs. They began to see themselves as owners of what they were only renting.

The cost

Finally the landlord decides he will ask his son, who is going back to the country, to visit and get what is due. He may have done this not just for convenience but because he recognized that someone with more authority than an agent was needed. It may be that he was thinking the son would have greater flexibility and power, and if there were genuine reasons for non-payment things could be sorted out on the spot.

But the tenants saw this as their great opportunity. They knew he was the landlord's only son and that if he were disposed of, the landlord would either be too grief-stricken or too busy searching for his son to bother with them. They probably thought at the time of the killing and the hiding of the body that they had won. But they had merely put off for a very short time the day of reckoning with the landlord. They had to appear in court, just as we will all have to do one day soon when we stand before the Judgement Seat of God.

This is why it was at this very point that Jesus turned to his listeners and asked them what the landlord should do. He was not going to condemn them. He didn't have to. They willingly condemned themselves.

What God wants

The story shows God's patience towards us. He sends reminder after gentle reminder of who he is and what is best for us. In all-embracing love he gives us a beautiful place to live and lets us use it freely, only asking that we look after his property. Eventually he has to send his only son to help us understand – and we kill him, or choose to ignore him, as we go our selfish way, abusing the very gifts that God has given us.

All God wants us to do is recognize and acknowledge what he has given us. This is enough for our redemption. Like the tenants, we know the difference between right and wrong. We know rent has to be paid and that we should respect what belongs to others. But so often we ignore this when it comes to the greatest gifts that God has sent for free. We want more than just to enjoy things for free. We want to possess them. They need to be 'mine'. The more that belongs to me, the more important I become in my own eyes. Like many animals, we need our own territory that we mark with our fancy gates, our flower beds and our personal space. We may even have our own 'turf' in our church, which can cause many unnecessary complications. Nations will even go to war over what is 'definitely theirs'.

How will we respond?

I want to challenge each of us individually. How different are we to these tenants? We have considerable freedoms. Yes, we do not have any say concerning the wealth of our parents or the size of the home into which we were born. But we do have choices concerning whether we are going to use the resources God gives us selfishly or for the greater good. The home that the landlord has built for us gives us great privileges but also brings with it some obligations – all of which God has equipped us to be able to cope with.

Have you shaken your comfort zone lately? Do you recognize that everything is God's? Jesus' challenge about how we live and how easily we take these things for granted hit home hard in his time and caused much resentment. Nothing has changed today. You will not hear this message coming from the main platforms at Christian conferences. After all, it might just offend us! These stories hit a raw nerve; they deeply challenge us and our first recourse is likely to be to try to shoot the messenger.

But if we put into action our belief that, as Psalm 24:1 tells us, 'the earth is the Lord's, and everything in it', we will enable God to break through and set us free from the power of selfish possession.

24. Fair Day's Work

Matthew 20:1–16

The Kingdom of heaven is like a gang-master who went out at 6 o'clock in the morning and hired some men and women to pick fruit. He agreed to pay them £100 for the day, then picked them up and drove them to the fruit farm.

At 9 o'clock he realized it was a bumper harvest and so he collected more workers. He offered to give them the right pay for the job. Because there was still an enormous amount of fruit to be picked, the gang-master repeated the same exercise at noon and at 3 p.m. Then, because all the fruit had to be gathered by 6 o'clock, he went out at 5 and was still able to find others who could help. He asked them, 'Why have you been standing around all day doing nothing?'

'Because no one has need of us,' they answered.

He said to them, 'Come, I can find work for you.'

When evening came the gang-master said to his foreman, 'Call the workers together and pay them their wages, beginning with the last ones hired and going back to those I took on first.'

The workers who were only hired at 5 p.m. came first, and the foreman gave each of them £100. So when those who had been hired first and had worked for longer hours came for their money, they expected to be paid more. But each of them also received £100. When they checked their money they began to grumble and complain about the gang-master. 'Those workers only worked for one hour,' they moaned, 'yet you have made them equal to us who have been sweating throughout the heat of the day doing this tiring work.'

But the gang-master heard them and said, 'Friends, I am not being unfair to you. Didn't we have an agreement that you would work for £100? So take your pay and go. It's a fair wage. But I want to give the people who were hired last the same as I gave to you. Don't I have the right to do as I want with my own money? Or is it that you are envious of my generosity?'

God's priorities turn the world's values upside down.

It's not fair!

How often, I wonder, have we heard the words 'It's not fair' spoken by a child when they think that someone else has got a newer, bigger or better toy than they have. As adults and as Christians, we are of course far too mature ever to think like that. Or are we?!

We have strong beliefs when it comes to fair play and will often protest strongly when we see real or perceived bias or unfairness. So questions like 'What is a fair wage?' or 'Is our taxation system fair?' are good questions. However, if we are being really honest with ourselves we will recognize that often we define the fairness of something in terms of how it directly affects us. We even tend to vote with our wallets.

This is why when Jesus told his parables, his audience would feel uncomfortable because they realized that what was being addressed was their self-centredness. We too must realize this, so if we do not feel unsettled when we read the parables we have almost certainly missed the point!

As with much 'casual' work today, workers in Jesus' time would be employed by the day and would receive their wages at the end of that day. 'Do not take advantage of a hired man who is poor and needy, whether he is a brother Israelite or an alien living in one of your towns. Pay him his wages each day before sunset, because he is poor and is counting on it. Otherwise he may cry to the Lord against you, and you will be guilty of sin,' said the Old Testament law (Deuteronomy 24:14–15). The workers all lived on the edge of destitution, having a hand-to-mouth existence and needing work every day just to survive.

There are certain times of the year when this story would have been relevant in Palestine, and there are equally times when it applies to some people in the UK. At harvest time the weather is beginning to change. Rains can come and cause problems. If the fruit is picked too early, it will not be ripe. If it is left too late, the frosts may come and destroy it.

It is often a race against the clock to get things gathered in on time, so workers are needed urgently. The days are also drawing in, and at fruit-picking time the work has to stop when it gets dark at around 6 o'clock.

Gangs of workers, often from abroad, make themselves available for such work at this time. This parable starts with the gang-master taking some of the workers to the fruit fields at the crack of dawn. He has offered them a fair rate for the day's work and they are all satisfied with the sum they will get at the end of the day. Several times during the day the gang-master realizes that he needs more workers to get the job done on time, so he goes and gets more workers. All are promised 'a fair wage'. They obviously feel in a less favourable position than the workers already hired, but at least they know they are going to have some money to take home for their families. By the time the last workers were hired, the shadows would already be lengthening, and it is likely that they would have been able to do very little work.

What motivated the gang-master to behave in this way? Why didn't he hire the entire workforce he needed at the start of the day? Maybe during the day he received a warning about the weather and realized that this could well be the last chance he would have of collecting all the fruit. Or as the day wore on and he noticed how much fruit was still left on the trees, he might have thought about those left behind who must have been feeling hopeless and afraid that they would have nothing to eat at the end of the day. Interestingly, before he hires them he checks to ensure that they genuinely want work and are not just idling around and expecting something for nothing. If they had been lazy they could have replied, 'It's too hot' or 'The system isn't fair'; but they replied, 'Because no one has need of us.'

They were desperate. The fact that they were still keen to work at 5 p.m., having been ready since 6 a.m., shows how much some pay, however little, was needed. These people did not belong to a trade union. They were not entitled to benefits. They relied entirely on chance employment. In some cases unscrupulous gang-masters would know that they were living in this country illegally and so would pay them a pittance. In these circumstances, losing just one day's pay would be critical.

So, at the end of the day, the workers who had only been there for one hour received their pay. Can you imagine their delight when they got what had been promised to those who had worked all day? And the other workers were delighted too – if those who had only worked one hour were given that sum, how much more would those who had worked longer get? Perhaps those who had worked twelve hours would get paid twelve times as much. But optimism soon turned to anxiety and then fear and anger as it became clear that it didn't matter how long you had worked: everybody was going to take home the same amount.

God's generosity

Imagine the outrage as this became obvious. 'It's simply not fair!' We, too, may sense that indignation. It seems to make little sense. What about an honest day's pay for an honest day's work?' Where's the justice in this? Surely this means we can lounge around all day and get as much as those who are working their socks off?

But the message is clear. The gang-master was being *fair* to those he had employed at the break of the day. But he was also being *generous* to those who had at first not been chosen. It is sometimes much easier for us to be fair than it is for us to be generous. We think of how things affect us and so easily condemn others. Either we are jealous of their good fortune ('How on earth he got that job I'll never know') or we lack sympathy for those who are hurting ('Why don't they just get off their backsides and get a job?').

We live in a reward and punishment world. We define justice as 'getting what you deserve'. But, thank God, the Gospel tells us that we do not get what we deserve! God instead forgives us and gives us what we need. And we are called to treat others in the same way.

It is easy to give the good child a reward for what they deserve. It is very difficult to give a reward to a child who is badly behaved, even when we know it is something they need. So this parable confronts our view on fairness and justice, because hope, mercy and compassion are included in it as well. It particularly upsets the religious, who believe they are deserving of special favour because they have been 'good' and kept the rules. Jesus happily mixed with sinners, even those who had not repented (Matthew 9:10–11). The thought of homeless dropouts and prostitutes being on the same footing in heaven is too much for the 'religious' to accept.

The dilemma

There is a clash here between the legalistic and the generous. Even if we accept that the gang-master can do what he likes with his money, who would be so foolish as to sign on at dawn the following day, knowing that if he only did one hour's work he would still be paid as much?

Similarly, if God welcomed some into heaven on the grounds of merit and others on the grounds of forgiveness, no one would know where they stood. So either everyone must work throughout their life and somehow 'win' their salvation or all must rejoice in the outrageous grace and forgiveness of our God. There can be no 'pick 'n' mix'. But the religious in every age seem to resent those who have been chosen when 'they don't deserve it'.

God's rewards

It is important to note right from the beginning of this story that those who worked all day long did receive the reward they were promised. Life is important and the way we live it does have consequences. But how these eventually affect our lives is down to God and not us. In our relationship with God we can only depend on his never-ending love. If we try to build a relationship with God, or for that matter with our neighbour, based on justice alone we are doomed before we start.

Yes, we can believe in the fairness of God. He sees the whole picture and will do what is right. But God is much more than fair. He is not some sort of accountant in the sky making sure that everything balances. The most unfair thing that has ever happened in history is the crucifixion of Jesus. He died for our failings, not for his. He died so we wouldn't get what we deserved. Instead, we got what we needed.

The lessons we need to learn

Just because we have been Christians all our lives or have led 'good' lives it does not mean that we are in any way superior to others – either in our churches or in our communities. God is always on the move, and new believers often have more passion to get things done for Christ as they realize what they have been set free from. Just like the workers who waited all day, desperate to know whether they would receive any help, so those who come to Jesus late in life may well have gone through many self-inflicted nightmares that the more mature Christian has been spared. It is not for us to judge.

This parable shows that there are no league tables of Christians. Our 'good works' cannot gain us promotion, although it is possible that by showing grace, love and compassion we will hear the words, 'Well done, good and faithful servant.'

God also demonstrates that he cares, and therefore that we are to care, about all aspects of life. Unemployment, for example, is a tragedy, and with very few jobs for life we should do what we can practically to help people when they are going through such awful things.

In this parable no one received less than they were entitled to receive. The only person who could have lost out financially was the gang-master himself. By being generous the gang-master may have had less money, but he would have received thanks from those who otherwise would have been starving.

And finally this parable tells us that *none* of us can earn what God gives us. What God gives us isn't a fair day's pay for a fair day's work. It is grace, love and forgiveness in abundance to all those who know Jesus as Lord. It is undeserved. It is in abundance. It is for evermore!

We cannot earn brownie points by saying to God, 'Look at my prayers. Look at my works!' This is belittling the very gift of Jesus himself. Yet it is so easy for the Pharisee to live within us. We work, in the final analysis, not for pay but to glorify God and to help others in some capacity. With this motivation we will see a reward we don't deserve. By sacrificing on earth for the benefits of others we will see great rewards in heaven, while others who have kept many things for themselves on earth will not have these friendships or thanks in heaven. It is this paradox that Jesus refers to. Those who look for rewards on earth will lose them, while those who concentrate on others will receive eternal blessing.

So let us rejoice when 'sinners' repent and when others come to Christ. Let us show God's unconditional love, even to those who seem a million miles from where God would want them to be. Let us be Jesus to them so that they too can experience this undeserved generosity.

25. In it for the Long Haul

Matthew 13:1–19 and 18–23

This is such a powerful story, and the analogy of the soils is so strong, I have taken the liberty of telling it twice! I hope you will forgive me.

A new manager was appointed to a football club. The appointment was featured extensively in the press and everyone was encouraged to support the team as it was hoped that they would do well. Some people, however, were cynical and rejected the manager. They talked amongst themselves and expected the team to perform no better than previously. After all, how can a new leader really change the way the team plays? Others, although agreeing it was a good appointment, went to the opening game and a home defeat saw them vowing never to return to watch such rubbish. Quite a few went to the first few games but soon got tempted away by other attractions or were put off by the cost of following the team. But the loyal supporters bought season tickets and followed the team resolutely through both good and bad games. They were rewarded when their team reached the Cup Final. As season ticket holders, they were able to get great seats and they celebrated as their team won a victory that will never be forgotten.

Those who refused outright to accept the new manager missed the fact that his coming was good news and didn't give him a chance. Their cynicism destroyed their judgement. Those who attended the first match had accepted that the coming of the manager was good news but as soon as something didn't quite go as they had hoped, the commitment disappeared. Those that went to the first few matches but then found other things to do were just fair-weather supporters. They claimed to be supporters when the team was doing well but weren't supportive when the results went badly. The season ticket holders on the other hand were committed to their team through rain or shine. They put the team first and were grateful to the manager for the results he got out of his team. For them, the final victory celebrations will last forever.

When it comes to our faith, are we all-weather supporters? Do we follow Jesus unswervingly whatever is happening: when we are being ridiculed or prayer has not been answered in the way that we had been hoping?

The following version is very similar to the original telling by Jesus. Given that farming is widespread, it is still very helpful and I have therefore retold it with few changes. Like the story, the message is profound and never changing.

A farmer went out to sow his seed. As he was doing so, some seed blew onto the path and the birds came and quickly ate it up. Some blew onto the unploughed areas at the edge of the fields where there was not much soil. The crop sprang up quickly because the soil was shallow. But as soon as the sun got hot, the plants became dried up and they quickly withered, as they had no roots. Other seeds blew onto the wasteland nearby where there were many thistles and nettles. They choked the plants and prevented them from growing. But other seed fell onto the good soil where it produced an enormous crop – up to a hundred times what was sown.

This is what the parable of the farmer means. When anyone hears the good news about Jesus and yet fails to grasp just what his coming to earth means, then the evil one comes along and blows the truth away. This is the seed that ends up on the path. The seed that fell on the unploughed areas is like the person who hears the message and accepts it with joy. However, because the person's faith has no real depth, the commitment lasts for only a short time. As soon as the first questions arise, some pressure arises, or he is laughed at for believing, he will turn away. The seed that fell among the nettles is like the person who heard the good news, but the constant focus on the here and now, and particularly the greedy desires for treasures on earth choke out the message and make it too challenging. But the seed that fell on good soil is like the person who hears the Good News and truly understands it. As a result of him putting the Kingdom first, the person grows strong in their faith, yielding up to one hundred times as much as was sown.

Understanding God's words

Last year I was speaking at a church and three people came up to me before the service and asked how I was. Unusually for me, I felt slightly under the weather so I replied 'Well, actually, I have a headache.' Two of the three said, 'Oh good'!

The point of this anecdote is to ask: Do we really listen? How much do we take in of what is being said to us? When a friend is telling us something, how long is it before our eyes glaze over? When do we start thinking about our problems, the need to get back to work or be at home in time for the soaps?

Companies actually adopt selling techniques of having several different people writing or phoning with a similar message. They understand that often we may have to hear the same message many times before it really begins to sink in. This is precisely why advertisements regularly repeat the same little phrase so often that it becomes ingrained in our memories: You should 'have a break; have a Kit Kat' or maybe it will be a Mars bar because 'a Mars a day helps you work, rest and play'. Whichever one it is, you know you deserve one 'because you're worth it'!

Really hearing and understanding what is actually being said is a very difficult thing to learn. Even if several of us hear the same talk, we may come away with totally different interpretations. This has a lot to do with our characters. We are also very good at 'listening' *for* other people. The number of times I have been at a talk and thought '*I wish my wife could hear that!*' Even worse, I may be secretly hoping that as she sits next to me she is squirming because what has just been said totally justifies my stance on something. I may, of course, not have heard the ten things that proved my perspective was ridiculous.

So, when we listen, do we pick up on what is really being said? Have we picked up the emotions that are running either at or just below the surface? Do we respond so the person talking to us knows that we haven't just been listening superficially but have picked up what was really being said?

A question of response

In this parable, what is being said is always the same – the seed is the same but the ground on which it falls is different and so there are different outcomes. So, the story is not about the Good News – that never changes – it is about us, and how we respond when we hear the story of Jesus. The different soils represent the different sort of responses we can make to what Jesus is offering. What has happened to us, what we add to it in life and what our priorities really are, affect the way we respond, just as the different types of soil caused different reactions when the seed was planted.

The seed on the path

Any seed on the path will stay on the surface, as the path will be hard and the seed will find it impossible to enter the ground to germinate. The seeds will just blow about on the surface and make a good meal for the passing birds.

This hardness is reflected in the listener who is hard of heart. He has already made his mind up. He knows better. There can be no God. When we die, we die. His barriers are so high and so strong that whatever happens, it can be rationally explained away.

We need to remember that, even as Christians, we can resort to this type. God is relevant to us all, even as our culture changes. Yet we can get stuck with certain things we hold dear to us to such an extent that they take us over and soon our rituals or opinions become more important to us than Jesus.

Equally, we can be convicted that we should live in a certain way, but our hardness prevents us from doing what we know in our heart of hearts that we should.

The seed on the edges

Sometimes there is sufficient soil to start things off but it is not deep enough to be able to hold on to the seeds as they try and grow. Because they cannot sink into the soil, they cannot form strong roots. As soon as any heat is applied to them, they quickly shrivel up and die.

Similarly, people can be shallow. On the surface, everything looks great but underneath not much is going on. Things such as prayer, fellowship and the reading of God's word aren't being done to help sustain the message and help it sink in. We cannot simply hear God's message, accept it and do nothing with it. It is, by far, the greatest news we will ever hear. It cries out for a response of joy and commitment. Simply to accept it but not let it affect every aspect of our life will soon mean that, in reality, the message is increasingly rejected and so will not last long at all.

Many people in Britain today would call themselves Christian. They have possibly been baptized or married in a church and they may have a basic understanding of who Jesus is. They may even acknowledge that he is the Son of God. But the fact that he died an agonizing death on the cross so they may know eternal life makes no difference to them whatsoever. They carry on as if this has no purpose or significance in 'real, everyday life'.

The seed in the nettles

Here Jesus is telling us that we often try to 'mix and match'. Good seed is planted but it is in soil where there are weeds and nettles. Both begin to grow but eventually the weeds crowd out the good plants and they can no longer be seen because of the taller weeds. Today, many things clamour for our attention. Time is a really precious commodity. Jesus mentions pleasure, wealth and things that worry us, specifically, but there are many other examples. Even as Christians, we may get so busy doing things for Jesus that we have less time to be with him, enjoy his company and hear what he has to say to us.

Others may hear the word of God and enthusiastically respond to it, just as if it is their latest 'hobby'. But the message of Jesus needs to be given absolute priority and made central in every aspect of our lives. Competing agendas and rival commitments soon mean that we begin to worship other things again. What are our idols today? What do we worship every day? Is it our new car, the extra furniture for the house? Is it the promotion we have been yearning for or the big salary increase we have 'deserved' for so long? I can't speak for you but, as I write this, I recognize that I need to do some weeding in my own life.

The seed in the good soil

Whenever seed is planted in good soil we see a very healthy response – often, as Jesus says, bearing a hundredfold return. But the key to this, again, is how we respond on hearing the message. Do we grasp the enormity of what Jesus has done for us? Are we prepared to let this 'seed' totally take over our lives? Are we happy to let God weed out the thistles and nettles that have grown there and apologize to God as and when some try and return?

In some ways, there are all these different types of soil in each one of us. Various pressures at differing times in our lives can affect us all. But we can rest assured in the good seed of this message, and as we follow Jesus more closely day by day, there will be more and more good soil within us.

Being good soil

As we continue to put Christ first, we know that our problems and faults will not just vanish overnight. In most cases, we have to give God permission to dig and break through our hard areas, work on the rough edges we would much rather keep hidden and weed out the nettles that can bind us and sting others.

Just as God loves us, so he loves others. By being good soil we can appear attractive to others and help them receive the same love, forgiveness and joy that he has so wonderfully given to us.

Conclusion

I hope you have enjoyed reading the parables and have gained fresh revelation of what Jesus is saying through them. Though the examples have changed, I hope you will see the eternal relevance of the truths that lie behind the stories.

These stories are full of inspiration about the world to come, but they are also told to help us keep thinking about God on earth. We are repeatedly called to be fully involved with the world, not to hide away in the 'safety' of our small Christian conclaves. It is important that we do not fear men and women and what they might say about us. Rather we should show by our actions that we believe in a wonderful, loving God. Furthermore we need to show by the power of the Holy Spirit not only that Jesus has set us free from our past mistakes and failings, but also that because of his death we will live for ever.

I leave you with these questions:

- Have you fully grasped what Jesus has done for *you*?
- Is the joy of that outrageous love bubbling out from you?

- Do you live out your faith in your everyday life?
- Are you more concerned about your responsibilities than your rights?
- Do you avoid being 'religious'?
- Do you look at the plank in your own eye and ignore the speck in others'?
- Are you more interested in others' needs than in your wants?
- Do God, others and heaven come before money, possessions and life on earth?

If you are beginning to answer yes to these questions, you are demonstrating that you have grasped what Jesus is saying to us through the parables!

May God bless you, and may you one day hear those wonderful words, 'Well done! You have been good and faithful.'